the Praying Rosary

*a journey
through scripture
and art*

Denis McBride CSsR

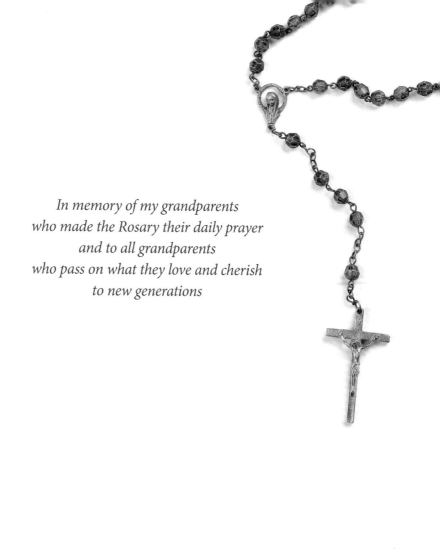

In memory of my grandparents
who made the Rosary their daily prayer
and to all grandparents
who pass on what they love and cherish
to new generations

Published by **Redemptorist Publications**
Alphonsus House,
Chawton, Hampshire,
GU34 3HQ, UK
Tel. +44 (0)1420 88222
Fax. +44 (0)1420 88805
Email rp@rpbooks.co.uk
www.rpbooks.co.uk

A registered charity limited by guarantee
Registered in England 3261721

Edited by Sr Janet Fearns
Designed by Eliana Thompson

ISBN 978-0-85231-415-9

Nihil Obstat: Rev William Wilson, Censor deputatus
Imprimatur: + Rt Rev Philip A Egan BA, STL, PhD
Bishop of Portsmouth, 1st September 2014

The Nihil Obstat and Imprimatur are official declarations that a book or pamphlet is free of doctrinal or moral error. No implication is contained therein that those who have granted the Nihil Obstat and Imprimatur agree with the contents, opinions or statements expressed.

Excerpts from THE JERUSALEM BIBLE, copyright © 1966 by Darton, Longman & Todd, Ltd and Doubleday, a division of Random House, Inc. Reprinted by permission.

Excerpts from THE CATECHISM OF THE CATHOLIC CHURCH, English Translation © Geoffrey Chapman, Libreria Editrice Vaticana, a Cassell imprint, 1999.

The Publisher gratefully acknowledges permission to use the following copyright material: extract taken from "Weighing In", taken from The Spirit Level © Estate of Seamus Heaney and reprinted by permission of Faber and Faber Ltd (Worldwide English language rights excluding US); David Scott: "The Priest in the Pulpit" from Beyond the Drift: New and Selected Poems, Bloodaxe Books, 2015; from "Conamara Blues" by John O'Donohue, published by Vintage, reprinted by permission of The Random House Group Ltd.

The publisher gratefully acknowledges permission to use the following material: maps on pp 9 and 105: courtesy of Truthandpurpose.com with topology data provided by Google, Mapa GI Israel and ORIEN-ME; map on p 41: courtesy of Bible History Online; maps on p 73 and back cover: courtesy of Holy Gospels in One provided by www.nakedlife.org.

The publisher has made all reasonable effort to trace copyright holders and any omissions will be corrected at reprint.

Cover image: Virgin of the Immaculate Conception (Seville Cathedral); sculpture attributed to Juan Martínez Montañes (1568-1649).

Printed by Bishops Printers Limited, Portsmouth PO6 1TR

Contents

Introduction

The beauty of the Rosary is that it is a leisurely journey, through twenty episodes, of the lives of Jesus and Mary. Apart from one decade, the four sets of five mysteries focus directly on Jesus and Mary as the principal characters in the ongoing drama. Jesus' story starts with the annunciation of his birth to Mary and concludes with his return to heaven, mission completed, in the ascension. Mary's story begins in the small village of Nazareth with the annunciation of the birth of Jesus and draws to a close dramatically, mission completed, in her assumption and coronation as queen in heaven.

Not surprisingly for this mother and son, both the Mary and Jesus stories begin and end in the same place.

The prayers of each decade – the Our Father, ten Hail Marys and the Glory Be – are repetitive and easily remembered, freeing the mind to reflect on the particular mystery. Like the ancient Hindu mantras, the steady repetition of the spoken words or sounds is meant to lead to awakening and enlightenment. The recurrent prayers of the Rosary are a vehicle leading not only to a deeper understanding of the mysteries but, more importantly, to a closer relationship with Jesus and Mary. The point of the Rosary is that we connect our own lives, whatever we are celebrating or enduring at the time of prayer, to the lives of Jesus and Mary.

In praying the Rosary, unburdened from remembering the actual prayers we say, we are invited to place ourselves in each scene, imagining the people, the places, the sights, the sounds, and the emotions that might be experienced during that actual event. We could decide to look at each scene from the point of view of a particular participant or an onlooker who happens upon it.

I remember my mother, who had a refined sympathetic imagination, saying to me once about the parable of the Prodigal Son: "Yes, but how would you feel about it all if you were the fatted calf? You'd hardly be cheering the returning son, would you?" Her instinct was always to go to the margins of a story; look and listen; then look again.

Meditating on the Rosary we are invited to look and listen; then look again. We are encouraged not only to say the prayers but go beyond recital and enter the beauty and complexity of the drama. Praying the Rosary presupposes that what is remembered is not lost history but an abiding force that continues to give meaning to what is happening now in our lives. The story of Jesus and Mary is part of our own lives: our story, in turn, is significant to them.

The format of this book is simple:

1. First there is a reading from the New Testament
2. This is followed by a meditation on the scripture passage
3. A painting is then included which offers its own take on the subject
4. There is a brief reflection on the painting
5. Finally there is a prayer on some aspect of the mystery.

My hope is that these reflections will be a real support to you in praying the Rosary and help you, in some small way, to grow personally closer to the loving lives of Jesus and Mary.

Finally I would like to record my sincere thanks to Eliana Thompson, our creative designer at Redemptorist Publications here in Chawton, for her wonderful work on the design of this book.

Denis McBride CSsR

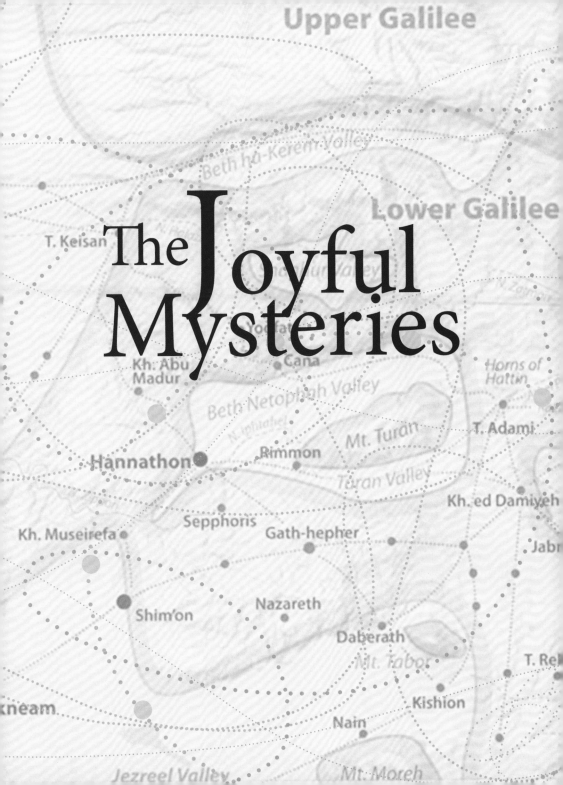

The Joyful Mysteries

The Annunciation

The Visitation

The Nativity

The Presentation
of Jesus in the Temple

The Finding of Jesus
in the Temple

The Annunciation

In the sixth month the angel Gabriel was sent by God to a town in Galilee called Nazareth, to a virgin betrothed to a man named Joseph, of the House of David; and the virgin's name was Mary. He went in and said to her, "Rejoice, so highly favoured! The Lord is with you." She was deeply disturbed by these words and asked herself what this greeting could mean, but the angel said to her, "Mary, do not be afraid; you have won God's favour. Listen! You are to conceive and bear a son, and you must name him Jesus. He will be great and will be called Son of the Most High. The Lord God will give him the throne of his ancestor David; he will rule over the House of Jacob for ever and his reign will have no end."

Mary said to the angel, "But how can this come about, since I am a virgin?" "The Holy Spirit will come upon you," the angel answered, "and the power of the Most High will cover you with its shadow. And so the child will be holy and will be called Son of God. Know this too: your kinswoman Elizabeth has, in her old age, herself conceived a son, and she whom people called barren is now in her sixth month, for nothing is impossible to God."

"I am the handmaid of the Lord," said Mary, "let what you have said be done to me." And the angel left her.

(Luke 1:26-38)

A life interrupted

We meet Mary for the first time when her life is dramatically interrupted by something she could not have imagined. The young Mary is neither yearning nor praying for a child: she is waiting to move in with her husband, at which point their marriage will be completed. Luke's story of the annunciation celebrates the initiative of God: the focus is on the surprise appearance of God's messenger and the message, not on the need or aspirations of Mary. This birth proposal is God's original idea. This child comes, not as a couple's answer to prayer, but as the gratuitous act of God.

Will Mary stay with her own domestic plans or risk an uncharted adventure as God's co-worker? Whatever Mary was planning for her life with Joseph, it did not include becoming pregnant outside that relationship. If she ever dreamed of being a princess, she knows that, as a peasant girl, she is destined to marry a carpenter. Mary welcomes the unforeseen and adjusts her life to this new adventure.

Mary responds by making her annunciation: to hand over her body and spirit to God's purpose. For the story of Jesus to be told, it needs more than God's word to be spoken: it also needs the human word to say, "Yes". That is why there are two annunciations: God's annunciation to Mary and Mary's annunciation to God. God's best plans for us can only happen when there is human co-operation, when God's word and our word come together. When those two annunciations coincide, God's word always takes flesh.

But how do you walk on an unmapped road with confidence? There are no antique maps, previously charted, to guide you on the way. There are no people to consult who have experienced the challenge you are now facing, no experts to guide you with their shared wisdom.

Sometimes the only way we can learn is by doing, setting out, leaving our cautious questioning behind us, even though we might still be afraid of our own inexperience and inadequacy. There is no rehearsal, we know, only live performance. We have to trust this new voice, a voice that we have discovered is truly ours, and head out to welcome the unforeseen. And we might know that we are not wholly alone in this new adventure.

At the beginning of his Gospel, Luke celebrates the fact that something radically new is about to take place. Because of God's initiative and a young girl's "Yes" to the unforeseen, the presence of God is going to become vulnerable in human flesh. In the ancient days it was the Ark of the Covenant that marked the presence of God. Now, Luke says, something new is going to happen. The presence of God will take human shape in the womb of Mary. Mary of Nazareth is the tabernacle of God.

John Collier, *The Annunciation*

Welcoming the unforeseen

One of America's most honoured artists, John Collier, was chosen as the chief sculptor for the Catholic Memorial at Ground Zero at the former World Trade Centre in New York. While much of his life has been spent making art for the world's major secular institutions and for private collectors, he now devotes his time to painting and sculpting for the Church.

Like the Old Masters before him, he sets the scene at the time of painting, not at the time of the event. This is not Nazareth in the ancient world but suburbia in today's world. The artist wanted to avoid the traditional view of Mary, dressed in the rich robes of the Renaissance, which keeps her at a safe distance and disguises her age. This Mary is a fourteen-year-old schoolgirl dressed in her blue and white uniform, wearing saddle shoes, with laces untied. Although the door behind her is closed, she stands on the welcome mat of her home.

Mary is interrupted on her own doorstep while dutifully reading. The artist has explained that she is reading from the book of the prophet Isaiah: "The Lord himself, therefore, will give you a sign. It is this: the maiden is with child and will soon give birth to a son whom she will call Immanuel" (Isaiah 7:14). Will Mary become this scripture?

Mary looks more puzzled than frightened by her deferential visitor with a neat haircut, whose full robe fashionably matches his wings. Does she suspect, perhaps, that he has arrived at the wrong address? This young girl is the picture of suburban serenity. If she is worried about what the neighbours will think, she does not show it. Gabriel has just delivered the large pot of lily flowers, signifying purity, which are about to blossom. On a nearby roof, a dove, symbolising the Holy Spirit, awaits the outcome. Collier manages to depict with unusual tenderness both the ordinariness of the setting and the extraordinariness of the event.

Prayer
Loving and tender Father,
we pray that we might attend your call
with a fraction of the generosity of Mary.

Even when we know
that we do not know
where the road will end,
what we will confront on the way
and can only guess how we will manage.

Even when we wonder
did we say "yes" too quickly, agree too readily?
Should we have asked more questions?
Should we have insisted on more guidance?
Will there be a way back to the uncomplicated life
we left behind us, before we heard your voice?

Forgive our questions, loving Father.
Teach us to be generous-hearted
when we hear your call
and to be trustful of your kind purposes,
knowing that, in following you,
we will never journey beyond your shadow.

The Visitation

Mary set out at that time and went as quickly as she could to a town in the hill country of Judah. She went into Zechariah's house and greeted Elizabeth.

Now as soon as Elizabeth heard Mary's greeting, the child leapt in her womb and Elizabeth was filled with the Holy Spirit. She gave a loud cry and said, "Of all women, you are the most blessed and blessed is the fruit of your womb. Why should I be honoured with a visit from the mother of my Lord? For the moment your greeting reached my ears, the child in my womb leapt for joy. Yes, blessed is she who believed that the promise made by the Lord would be fulfilled."

(Luke 1:39-45)

Celebrating motherhood

Luke opens his Gospel, not with the young, the bold and the strong, but with a dumb old priest and a pregnant old woman – Zechariah and Elizabeth. They have spent their married life praying for a child and their stubborn faith is rewarded with the gift of a son, John the Baptist. Elizabeth's unexpected pregnancy was given to Mary as a sign that nothing is impossible to God.

As one day Jesus will travel south from Nazareth to see John the Baptist in the wilderness of Judea, now Jesus' mother journeys south to the hills of Judea to see the mother of John the Baptist. Luke's account of Mary's visit brings together the two mothers who have been promised birth through divine intervention. Mary hurries to the home of her relative, Elizabeth, who has shyly been in hiding for five months: Mary's gracious visit brings the old woman out of seclusion.

This poignant scene of the meeting between Mary and Elizabeth is an enduring celebration of motherhood. The visitation is principally a story of two mothers: the young mother of Jesus, who was not expecting to become pregnant and the ancient mother of John the Baptist, who had prayed all her married life for this moment.

Their sons are important, but the visitation is not their story: in this narrative the men are secondary. However important the men will become, however heroic their lives, they will start life as we all did – waiting in the womb of our mother.

This Gospel passage celebrates the role of women in the birth of greatness and the simple truth that our lives are a gift from others.

- Before Jesus and John will carry others, they will first be carried and nurtured by women

- Before Jesus and John reach out to others, women will first minister to them

- Before Jesus and John cherish others, especially those who are poor and weak, women will first cherish them

For Luke, Elizabeth and Mary are not just individual characters: they represent the whole of scripture. Elizabeth comes out of the Old Testament, an old woman who has waited on the promises of God. It is not just that her time has come; the final time has now arrived in the last of the prophets, her son, John the Baptist. He will go before Jesus in birth, he will go before Jesus in life, and he will go before Jesus in death.

Mary, on the other hand, represents what is utterly fresh and startling, personifying God's new beginning: from her womb will come the saviour of all humanity. She makes a journey to meet old Israel. The New Testament crosses the divide and journeys to meet the Old. The Old Testament and the New Testament embrace in loving recognition. This new time begins with womb-shaking rejoicing.

The Magdeburg Ivories, *The Visitation*

"Two women locked in the story of birth"

Otto the Great, credited with being the first Holy Roman Emperor, commissioned a large number of ivory plaques depicting scenes from the life of Christ. Originally there were fifty to sixty of them, all carved in workshops in Milan. The occasion was the celebration of the new archbishopric in AD 968 and its cathedral of Magdeburg, west of modern Berlin.

Sixteen of the ivories still survive. One of the most powerful and engaging depicts the visitation, showing the strong figures of Mary and Elizabeth in a geometric enclosure with a pierced background. The figures look monumental, somewhat stiff, their faces and the drapery of their clothes almost identical. They have their noses pressed together in greeting, their eyes fixed in mutual recognition. They hold on to each other, perhaps expressing their need of each other's support.

As they lean into one another, Mary, on the right, clasps Elizabeth on the back while she discreetly moves her left hand over Elizabeth's growing globe – as if to determine for herself Gabriel's assurance that, "she whom people called barren is now in her sixth month." Mary's delicate touch gives an added reason why the child John should make a joyful leap in Elizabeth's womb.

John O'Donohue catches the biblical meeting well, imagining the moment Mary and Elizabeth meet:

> Two women locked in the story of birth.
> Each mirrors the secret the other heard.
>
> John O' Donohue, *Conamara Blues*

In the ivory plaque you can see, graphically depicted, "two women locked in the story of birth" as "each mirrors the secret the other heard." They also mirror one another, these two pregnant mothers, favoured by God to further the story of salvation.

Prayer

For your choice of Elizabeth,
pregnant much later than she dreamed;
for your choice of Mary,
pregnant much sooner than she expected:
we bless you, Father, with a full heart.

We pray for all pregnant mothers:
that they may be secure and safe
in heart and mind and body;
that they may be strengthened
for the responsibility ahead of them,
and know the consolation of loving support.

We pray for all mothers:
that they may always delight in the presence
of the children entrusted to their safe-keeping;
that they may be a shelter for them
and a source of love and wisdom.

For all children we pray:
that they may grow in the security of family life
and experience their dignity as children of God.
May they always stay connected to their parents
in true affection and respect.

The Nativity

Now at this time Caesar Augustus issued a decree for a census of the whole world to be taken. This census – the first – took place while Quirinius was governor of Syria, and everyone went to his own town to be registered. So Joseph set out from the town of Nazareth in Galilee and travelled up to Judaea, to the town of David called Bethlehem, since he was of David's House and line, in order to be registered together with Mary, his betrothed, who was with child. While they were there the time came for her to have her child, and she gave birth to a son, her first-born. She wrapped him in swaddling clothes, and laid him in a manger because there was no room for them at the inn.

In the countryside close by there were shepherds who lived in the fields and took it in turns to watch their flocks during the night. The angel of the Lord appeared to them and the glory of the Lord shone round them. They were terrified, but the angel said, "Do not be afraid. Listen, I bring you news of great joy, a joy to be shared by the whole people. Today in the town of David a saviour has been born to you; he is Christ the Lord. And here is a sign for you: you will find a baby wrapped in swaddling clothes and lying in a manger." And suddenly with the angel there was a great throng of the heavenly host, praising God and singing:

"Glory to God in the highest heaven,
and peace to men who enjoy his favour".

(Luke 2:1-14)

Celebrating new life

In reflecting on the birth of Jesus, we celebrate the gift of a unique child, the one whom we honour as the Son of God. In Luke's scene we behold supreme power in low profile. This is hosanna, not in the highest, but hosanna in the lowest. Jesus is not rootless, but is born a member of a specific tribe and people; he does not begin from zero, but enters an unfolding history between a yesterday and a tomorrow. He does not invent himself, but will discover himself as a unique link in a long line of faith. He is a Palestinian Jew born in the reign of Caesar Augustus and King Herod. He is in time and, therefore, in between times.

The birth of Jesus is located in space and time, the natural boundaries of every human life story. To be human is always to be "somewhere", never "nowhere": it is always to exist "some-time", never "no-time". "Once upon a time" is fairy-tale time: the reign of Augustus is real time. Luke registers the birth of Jesus as a sign of the historical reality of the visit of God. In the person of Jesus, God has visited his people. God has registered himself in a specific place and at a specific time: we celebrate this wonder.

We reverence the love of God which shows itself in the fragile bundle of the child Jesus and we celebrate our love of God through the person of Jesus. Perhaps it is true to say that we can love only what we can put our arms around. In order to love, we need a particular name, a particular face, a particular person. And we have God's particulars in Jesus. When we look at Jesus, we no longer have to guess at God: the best of what we know about God is revealed in Jesus. This little one is the icon of the living God. Like Mary and Joseph, we can all put our arms around this child from Bethlehem.

But the child will not stay a child. As my old Jesuit professor George McCauley wrote:

> The baby would grow up. He would take a lot of people to heart and suffer because of his love for others. He would take them to heart in their concise concrete humanity: their lopsided resolve, their pettiness and isolation, the spectres of guilt and violence that inhabit them, their unpredictable bodies and shrill memories, their jobs and lusts, their in-laws and thin aspirations. Sometimes his heart would look more like an infirmary than a treasure room. We may assume that his mother taught him a thing or two about love.

George McCauley, *The Unfinished Image*

We celebrate the beginning of Jesus' life because of what he became for us; we reverence his birth because of his death and resurrection. This child cannot be cloistered in the manger: the one who will love us to death is the one we celebrate at his birth.

Harry Clarke,
The Adoration of the Magi (detail)

Here to stay

There are two birth stories in the Gospels, one by Luke and the other by Matthew.

Luke's account is more familiar to us: the holy family leave their home in Nazareth, in Galilee; the northerners travel south to Bethlehem to register for the census. In the overcrowded town, Jesus is born in an emergency shelter and placed in a feeding-trough for animals, where he is visited by local shepherds.

In contrast, Matthew's account portrays Mary and Joseph as southerners, natives of Bethlehem: Jesus is born at home in the house of Joseph. Instead of the first visitors being local peasants, Matthew has aristocratic star-gazers, who enjoy ready access to King Herod's palace and the imperial court; these strangers have journeyed from the east, bringing their curious, expensive gifts.

The Irish artist Harry Clarke has delicately caught Matthew's exotic scene in his stained glass window. Clarke, who came from a Dublin family of church decorators, was an outstanding illustrator of books as well as an artist in stained glass and is celebrated for the finesse of his graphic drawing. He was clearly influenced by the Art Nouveau and Art Deco movements. His use of rich colours makes his work readily distinctive, mixing blues and purples and greens and yellows. His favourite colour is, clearly, deep blue.

In this scene, Mary is elegant and serene as she holds her beautiful child in her lap. Exquisitely bedecked and bejewelled, she is not outclassed by the finery of her visitors' attire. More importantly, she is utterly still and unfussed amidst this unexpected traffic. If contemplative thinking means accepting being where you are, Mary's open-eyed awareness speaks for itself: she is here to stay – unlike them. From this peaceful scene one would never guess the danger these visitors bring to this family and this town. For now, just for now, all is colour and light, gracefulness and charm.

Prayer

When the song of the angels has been stilled,
when the star has gone from the night sky,
when the kings have reached their far shores,
when the shepherds have returned to their flocks,
then the work of Jesus really begins.

As his followers we are pledged:
to find those who are lost;
to heal those who are broken in spirit;
to feed those who are hungry;
to release those who are oppressed;
to rebuild those torn by strife;
to bring peace among all peoples;
to bring the light of the Gospel
into the darkest corners of our world.

May the joy of the angels,
the eagerness of the shepherds,
the perseverance of the wise men,
the love of Joseph and Mary,
and the peace of the Christ child
be ours to share with all we meet.

The Presentation of Jesus in the Temple

And when the day came for them to be purified as laid down by the Law of Moses, Mary and Joseph took him up to Jerusalem to present him to the Lord – observing what stands written in the Law of the Lord: Every first-born male must be consecrated to the Lord – and also to offer in sacrifice, in accordance with what is said in the Law of the Lord, a pair of turtledoves or two young pigeons. Now in Jerusalem there was a man named Simeon. He was an upright and devout man; he looked forward to Israel's comforting and the Holy Spirit rested on him. It had been revealed to him by the Holy Spirit that he would not see death until he had set eyes on the Christ of the Lord. Prompted by the Spirit he came to the Temple; and when the parents brought in the child Jesus to do for him what the Law required, he took him into his arms and blessed God; and he said:

> "Now, Master, you can let your servant go in peace, just as you promised; because my eyes have seen the salvation which you have prepared for all the nations to see, a light to enlighten the pagans and the glory of your people Israel."

As the child's father and mother stood there wondering at the things that were being said about him, Simeon blessed them and said to Mary his mother, "You see this child: he is destined for the fall and for the rising of many in Israel, destined to be a sign that is rejected – and a sword will pierce your own soul too – so that the secret thoughts of many may be laid bare."

There was a prophetess also, Anna, the daughter of Phanuel, of the tribe of Asher. She was well on in years. Her days of girlhood over, she had been married for seven years before becoming a widow. She was now eighty-four years old and never left the Temple, serving God night and day with fasting and prayer. She came by just at that moment and began to praise God; and she spoke of the child to all who looked forward to the deliverance of Jerusalem.

(Luke 2:22-38)

When the old meets the new

The new family – Mary, Joseph and Jesus – leave their country home in the north, among the hills of Lower Galilee, and travel south to the city of Jerusalem. The northerners come south; the country folk head for the great religious centre, the city where Jesus will eventually face his appointment with death.

As an upright Jewish family, they want to honour the Law and consecrate their first-born son to the Lord. The family's destination is the Temple where they are welcomed by two ancient figures, the prophet Simeon and the prophetess Anna.

In spite of being an old man, Simeon looks forward, not backwards; he looks ahead to the consolation of Israel. He is not captivated by the past, the world that populates his memory, but is attentive to the present moment and what is yet to happen. With the visit of this new family, Simeon's waiting and faith are now rewarded: his mission is completed when he can see in this child the anointed of God.

So, we have the meeting between youth and old age; between the young mother and the old venerables; between promise and fulfilment, between waiting and completion. You watch Simeon take the child into his arms; you watch old age reach out for the flesh of a promise fulfilled, gathering this assurance into his quieting arms as he breaks into the poetry of the *Nunc Dimittis*. He celebrates something new: that this child is not only the glory of his own people, but is given as a gift to every nation on earth.

And Anna: she is the attentive woman who prays and waits and watches. Anna is always around the Temple, night and day. She makes herself God's neighbourhood watch with her energetic nose for what is happening in her neighbour's house. An inquisitive woman of faith, she is on permanent lookout: nothing is going to get past this alert sentinel. This vigilant eighty-four-year-old woman now carries the story to all who have been looking for the redemption of Jerusalem. The waiting of the ancients is now over; the Gospel begins.

As Mary fostered this child within her, so she now shares him with a waiting world. This child is her own, but not entirely her own: he is given, as Simeon prophesied, as a light to enlighten all peoples. That is why we celebrate Mary as a model for all Christians: we are challenged to carry Christ, not in wombs, but in hearts and minds, to carry him to those who have spent their lives waiting for the day when they can, at last, sense that good news is within their reach.

Andrea Mantegna, *The Presentation of Christ in the Temple*

A painful annunciation

In Simeon's personal address to Mary, not only does Mary hear that her son is destined to be rejected, but also that a sword will pierce her own soul. That is a very painful annunciation to hear about your son's future and your own. Mary will be seriously wounded because of her child, a truth captured exquisitely in Andrea Mantegna's painting.

As we look at the painting, we feel we have stumbled on a very private moment, spotted through an open window. We absorb the details. We notice that Simeon is not looking at the extraordinary child wrapped in swaddling clothes but at his mother: his eyes seem to drill through her like the words he has just spoken. Joseph, with furrowed brow, looks sternly at Simeon: they have not come to the Temple to hear such tormented prophecy. The two witnesses look away in hopeless politeness as if what they have just heard is too private and, therefore, best left unattended. Her right elbow anchored on the window as she holds her child, Mary lowers her eyes, pensively, looking at Simeon's closed lips – did he just say that? She has just heard something as personal as it is painful. We are left to wonder as we walk away.

This painting is an extraordinary insight into the conflict that is part of Mary's motherhood. While Gabriel told Zechariah that his son would be a joy and delight – every father's dream – Mary hears a different annunciation from Simeon: that her son will be like a sword driven through her soul – every mother's nightmare.

Mary hears two annunciations about her son: one from an angel that listed his future accomplishments; and now one from an old prophet, telling her that her son will be cast aside and she will be deeply wounded because of what happens to him. How do you hold these two annunciations together?

Prayer

We pray, dear Lord, in thanksgiving
that you were welcomed as a child
by Simeon and Anna in the Temple.

We pray for those who are old
yet stay alert to the gift of the present moment;
who turn away from living in the past of memory
to attend the startling new things you are doing
in the here and now of ordinary time.

We pray in thanksgiving especially
for old people who welcome the young
and encourage them with their love and wisdom.

We ask you, Lord, to abide with all your people
in the evening of their life.
Comfort them with the assurance of your presence;
grant that the failing powers of their body
may be matched by an increase of faith in you,
so that, trusting themselves to your mercy,
they may live in quiet confidence and peace.

The Finding of Jesus in the Temple

Every year Jesus' parents used to go to Jerusalem for the feast of the Passover. When he was twelve years old, they went up for the feast as usual. When they were on their way home after the celebrations, the boy Jesus stayed behind in Jerusalem without his parents knowing it. They assumed he was with the caravan. It was only after a day's journey that they went to look for him among their relations and acquaintances. When they failed to find him they went back to Jerusalem looking for him everywhere.

Three days later, they found him in the Temple, sitting among the doctors, listening to them, and asking them questions; and all those who heard him were astounded at his intelligence and his replies. They were overcome when they saw him, and his mother said to him, "My child, why have you done this to us? See how worried your father and I have been, looking for you." "Why were you looking for me?" he replied. "Did you not know that I must be busy with my Father's affairs?" But they did not understand what he meant.

He then went down with them and came to Nazareth and lived under their authority. His mother stored up all these things in her heart. And Jesus increased in wisdom, in stature, and in favour with God and men.

(Luke 2:41-52)

Lost and found

The Temple in Jerusalem provides the setting for our last decade of the Joyful Mysteries. As the Gospel tells us, Jesus was brought up in Nazareth by Mary and Joseph and, like a good Jewish son, lived under their wisdom and authority. From them he would have his first experience of being loved, of being held, of being heard and of being nurtured. He was a member of the extended Jewish family which, unlike our nuclear family, includes every kind of kinship, no matter how remote.

The scene opens with the journey from Nazareth up to the holy city of Jerusalem. Like many Palestinian Jews, Mary and Joseph would go every year, but this year is special because Jesus is now twelve years old. In later customs, the Jewish boy was introduced to adulthood when he was twelve – he became *bar mitzvah*, a son of the Law, assuming the responsibilities to which his parents had earlier committed him. In going to Jerusalem, it is possible that Jesus was celebrating an earlier form of this rite of passage: he was no longer a child; he had begun the process of being a man.

The story tells us that Jesus stayed behind in Jerusalem, a decision surprisingly unknown either to Mary or Joseph who had started travelling back to Nazareth: to modern parents this might appear negligent on the part of Joseph and Mary. On returning to Jerusalem, after three days, they find Jesus with the teachers in the Temple. He seems at home here, listening and answering questions, his insights provoking amazement. Previously, Luke has spoken of astonishment at what others have said of Jesus; now people are astonished at Jesus himself.

It also appears, however, that the sword that would pierce Mary's soul, prophesied earlier by Simeon, is already at work. Mary's question focuses on how anxious she and Joseph are: "See how worried your father and I have been, looking for you." Jesus' reply, however, focuses on his heavenly Father: "Did you not know that I must be busy with my Father's affairs?" Two different concerns bypass one another. The first words attributed to Jesus are spoken in the Temple and focus on his unique relationship with his Father: Jesus' first priority – his "I must" – is to do as his Father commands him. His identity and direction in life transcend family history.

Luke says that the parents of Jesus did not understand Jesus' saying, a reaction to Jesus' words which will happen throughout his later ministry. Luke adds, however, the familiar note that Mary "stored all these things in her heart".

Like all mothers do regarding their children, Mary will have much to store in her heart, not least what she does not understand about her son. As mothers have to let go of their child in the act of giving birth, so all mothers, including Mary, will have to let go of her son over and over again.

William Holman Hunt, *The Finding of the Saviour in the Temple* (detail)

Family differences

William Holman Hunt, a member of the Pre-Raphaelite Brotherhood, travelled to Israel in 1854, where he started this painting, but was to finish it only six years later in London. It is a work of sacred realism. It also portrays the artist's understanding that this is the moment when the young Jesus comes to a realisation of who he is and what his mission involves – the Son committed to do his Father's will.

Mary and Joseph interrupt the learned seminar their son is giving to the Doctors of the Law. For them, family takes precedence over learned discourses, even in this sacred place. Both are turned towards Jesus, their eyes fixed on him, their hands held together in protective custody over his right shoulder. While Mary looks utterly relieved as she leans into her son, the turbaned Joseph looks somewhat puzzled, his body erect. Perhaps the frayed red tassels falling from Mary's waist reflect her threadbare nerves.

For all the emphasis on family reunion, Jesus appears separate. His mother's question, "Why have you done this to us?" appears not to unsettle him. Although Jesus' left hand rests lightly on Mary's wrist, his look is not fixed on his family but focuses elsewhere. His right hand is tightening the red leather belt around his tunic, as if bracing himself for a journey that will take him away from sacred space and family. He has a calling beyond this place and time, other people to meet and other priorities to keep. His is the only head that is uncovered, his hair appearing as if lit from within.

In the background the sellers and money-changers are going about their business; a child is carried for consecration, a lamb for sacrifice. Outside the door of the Temple, a blind beggar sits, holding out his right hand; beyond him the builders work to complete this great structure; beyond the workers and the city can be seen the outline of the Mount of Olives where the passion of the adult Jesus will begin and where he will bind himself in prayer to do his Father's will.

Prayer

Lord Jesus Christ,
we bless you that you did not come to us
as a bolt from the blue
but as a child in your mother's womb;
that you did not cling to
your equality with God
but emptied yourself
and became as all men are,
even to accepting death on a cross.

We thank you for crowning our humanity
with the gift of a life lived for others.
We bless you for your struggle
to do your Father's will in all things,
even when it bewildered and hurt
those who were closest to you.

Help us to hallow the Father's name
and be open to do his will.
May we be steadfast in praying your prayer,
that our Father's will may be done on earth
as it is in heaven.

The Luminous Mysteries

The Baptism of Jesus

The Wedding at Cana

The Proclamation
of the Kingdom

The Transfiguration

The Institution
of the Eucharist

The Baptism of Jesus

And so it was that John the Baptist appeared in the wilderness, proclaiming a baptism of repentance for the forgiveness of sins. All Judaea and all the people of Jerusalem made their way to him and as they were baptised by him in the river Jordan they confessed their sins. John wore a garment of camel-skin and he lived on locusts and wild honey. In the course of his preaching he said, "Someone is following me, someone who is more powerful than I am, and I am not fit to kneel down and undo the strap of his sandals. I have baptised you with water, but he will baptise you with the Holy Spirit."

It was at this time that Jesus came from Nazareth in Galilee and was baptised in the Jordan by John. No sooner had he come out of the water than he saw the heavens torn apart and the Spirit, like a dove, descending on him. And a voice came from heaven, "You are my Son, the Beloved; my favour rests on you."

(Mark 1: 4-11)

Beginning after John

Mark opens his Gospel with a stage of conflict: all the people are leaving sacred space, the holy city of Jerusalem, and going out into ordinary space, the wilderness of Judea, to listen to John the Baptist. Usually pilgrimages go from ordinary space to sacred space: the reverse is now happening as people vote with their feet and travel out of the city to see the holy man in the desert. They believe that when they listen to John they can hear the accent of God.

In the first days of the early Church, Peter instructs Cornelius and offers the centurion a summary of the beginning of the Jesus story: "You must have heard about the recent happenings in Judaea; about Jesus of Nazareth and how he began in Galilee, after John had been preaching baptism. God had anointed him with the Holy Spirit and with power" (Acts 10:37-38).

As if observing Peter's instruction, Mark celebrates this beginning: the adult Jesus leaves home in Nazareth, travels south to the wilderness of Judea, joins the crowds and is baptised by John and anointed with the Spirit.

To understand the beginning of the story of the adult Jesus, the four Gospels point us to someone else, the figure of John the Baptist. This independent preacher is the prophetic force that stands between the hidden life of Jesus and his public ministry. Jesus does not begin alone: none of us does. Jesus' beginning is not a solitary event in a landscape empty of people: he begins at a public gathering, in the midst of the crowds who seek out the Baptist.

Like many others, Jesus is attracted by John's reputation and is moved to journey from his northern home in Nazareth to see this fiery reformer – the one who proclaims the word of God with authority, the one who attracts people from the holy city of Jerusalem and the surrounding region. After his public baptism, Jesus does not return to the settled life in Nazareth as a carpenter but will take a new direction as a wandering prophet and healer.

The local Palestinian scene of Jesus' baptism in the River Jordan suddenly becomes a cosmic realm as the heavens are rent open and God makes known the identity of Jesus to the reader. God's annunciation of Jesus' identity will remain normative for the remainder of the Gospel.

The focus on Jesus' baptism by John now shifts to his baptism by the Holy Spirit: God is present in his beloved Son, Jesus, who is empowered to do the work of God. This is a huge turning-point in the life of Jesus as he leaves his accustomed life behind and sets out on a wholly different journey.

The anointing of Jesus signals the beginning of his public ministry, one that will eventually lead to his death. He will later speak of his death when he addresses the sons of Zebedee: "Can you drink the cup that I must drink, or be baptised with the baptism with which I must be baptised?" (Mark 10:38). His public life on earth is bounded by his baptism in the Jordan and by his baptism on the cross.

Piero della Francesca, *The Baptism of Christ*

A wonderful beginning

The Baptism of Christ was Piero della Francesca's first great commission. It was painted around 1440, for the priory of Saint John the Baptist in Borgo San Sepolcro, his hometown in Tuscany, which can be glimpsed in the background. The painting was the centrepiece of a multi-panelled altar-piece, but now hangs by itself in the National Gallery, London.

The scene is beautifully lit: the central character is majestic and luminous, the vertical axis of the whole setting. The painting captures the moment when John the Baptist pours water over the head of Christ. This action is accompanied by three wonderful elements: the heavens opening, the appearance of the Holy Spirit in the form of a dove and the voice of God the Father identifying Jesus as his beloved Son.

The streaked clouds in the sky echo the perfectly horizontal dove; the foliage of the walnut tree provides a protective arch over the action of the baptism. John's face, in profile, looks on the full face of Jesus whose eyes are cast down introspectively. With his right hand John pours the water from the bowl with great delicacy, his nervousness shown as he pulls back his left lower leg and holds the parted fingers of his other hand stiffly. This John is fully aware of the greatness of the one who stands before him.

The three garlanded angels – two are seen holding onto each other – look on apprehensively as if they know where this story will lead: that Jesus will again end up naked except for a loincloth, but this time with his arms outstretched on a cross. In the background a young man disrobes for baptism, his white skin reflecting the body of Jesus: although Jesus is linked to heaven, he also shares our bodily humanity. Through the arched body of the young man you can catch a glimpse of three of the overdressed officials – clearly they are not readying themselves for baptism. Unlike the principal characters, these enemies of Jesus cast shadows at his baptism as they will surely do at his death.

47

Prayer

Almighty God,
who sent your servant John the Baptist
to call people to a new way of life
and to prepare for the coming of the Lord:
we bless you for the authority of his witness
and the integrity of his life,
praying that we, in our turn,
might lead others into the presence of your Son.

At the baptism of Jesus in the River Jordan
you anointed him in the power of the Holy Spirit
and revealed him to be your Beloved Son
on whom your favour rests.

Grant that we who are baptised into his name
may dedicate our lives to your service
and be found worthy of our calling.

Everlasting and gracious Father,
sanctify us by the same Spirit,
that we may proclaim the liberating power of the Gospel
by acts of love in your name.

Immerse us in your grace
and guide our lives to live our baptismal vows
empowered by the Holy Spirit
and the example of Christ our Lord,
in whose name we pray.

The Wedding at Cana

Three days later there was a wedding at Cana in Galilee. The mother of Jesus was there, and Jesus and his disciples had also been invited. When they ran out of wine, since the wine provided for the wedding was all finished, the mother of Jesus said to him, "They have no wine." Jesus said, "Woman, why turn to me? My hour has not come yet." His mother said to the servants, "Do whatever he tells you."

There were six stone water jars standing there, meant for the ablutions that are customary among the Jews: each could hold twenty or thirty gallons. Jesus said to the servants, "Fill the jars with water," and they filled them to the brim. "Draw some out now," he told them, "and take it to the steward." They did this; the steward tasted the water, and it had turned into wine.

Having no idea where it came from – only the servants who had drawn the water knew – the steward called the bridegroom and said, "People generally serve the best wine first, and keep the cheaper sort till the guests have had plenty to drink; but you have kept the best wine till now."

This was the first of the signs given by Jesus: it was given at Cana in Galilee. He let his glory be seen, and his disciples believed in him.

(John 2:1-11)

The unexpected gift

Running out of wine at a wedding feast is hardly a life-or-death situation: inconvenient and embarrassing, yes, but not an enduring calamity, except that the family's shame might eclipse other memories of the feast. In his Gospel, John chooses this troubled domestic scene to celebrate the story of Jesus' first great sign, one that reveals his glory and leads the disciples to believe in him.

The evangelist introduces the mother of Jesus first – he never calls her Mary. Like the beloved disciple in this Gospel, the mother of Jesus remains unnamed, perhaps emphasising their unique relationship to Jesus. John then tells us that Jesus and the disciples have also been invited. Perhaps this is the wedding of one of Mary's close relatives, which would naturally make her more sensitive to the distressing news that the couple have run out of wine. Mary simply informs Jesus of the situation without suggesting a remedy or asking him to do anything.

Jesus' reply underlines the point that he cannot be bound by family relationships, but only by his Father's will: his mission has priority over the agenda of his kinsfolk.

This is reminiscent of Luke's account of the twelve year-old Jesus in the Temple who responds to his mother by saying: "Did you not know that I must be busy with my Father's affairs?" (Luke 2:49). In the language of John, the adult Jesus now says that his hour has not yet come. Undaunted by her son's reply, Mary instructs the servants to do whatever Jesus tells them. It seems strange for a guest to instruct the household servants, but if Mary is a close family relative, this would not be out of place.

Clearly Mary expects her son to rise to the occasion, believing that he can turn poverty into plenty.

While there is no wine, there is an abundance of water in six stone jars for the Jewish ritual of purification. Jesus decides to save this distressing situation and tells the servants to fill these to the brim; after doing this they discover that the water has been changed into wine – all one hundred and twenty gallons. When the steward tastes it, he compliments the bridegroom for keeping the best wine until last – an unusual practice for wedding feasts which could last for days.

The story gives us a marvellous image of the loving relationship we have with God through Jesus. Jesus is ungrudging and bountiful in the gifts he offers. As John wrote in the Prologue to his Gospel: "Indeed, from his fullness we have, all of us, received" (John 1:16). This is demonstrated beautifully at the wedding feast when Jesus offers not a carafe of *vin ordinaire* but gallons of the finest vintage. With him there is always plenty.

Master of the Catholic Kings, *The Marriage at Cana* (detail)

With him there is always plenty

Completed around 1495 by an unidentified Spanish artist, celebrated as the Master of the Catholic Kings, this painting now hangs in the National Gallery of Art in Washington, DC. The artist's title is derived from his principal work, *The Altarpiece of the Catholic Kings*, of which this panel is a part. The whole piece was completed during the reign of the Catholic monarchs, King Ferdinand and Queen Isabella.

The stylish setting and the elegant costumes are Spanish, reflecting the time of the painting, and you can see the artist's energy and meticulous skill in documenting the domestic details. At the wedding table, Jesus raises his right hand in benediction over the six jars on the tiled floor in front of him, while Mary joins her hands in prayer in recognition of the miracle. The governor of the feast, sitting between Jesus and the bridegroom, looks sceptical as he holds a tasting cup of the new wine which has just been passed to him by the boy-servant on the left. With down-turned mouth the governor stares at the servant who returns his scrutiny with surprising confidence.

The boy-servant on the right (is he a twin?) offers a goblet of the new wine to the bridal pair, indicating with his left hand that this offering is the unexpected gift provided by Jesus. The aristocratic bride and groom lower their eyes in reverent acceptance of the divine gift. In the background you catch a glimpse through an open door of their marriage bed, where two white pillows lie neatly arranged on the red bedcover.

In contrast to the restrained politeness in the painting's foreground, behind the head of Jesus you get a glimpse into the kitchen, where an elderly servant has no misgivings about the quality of the new wine as he tips a flagon of this unique vintage into his mouth. The servants have caught the spirit of the occasion: this is a time for unbridled rejoicing.

Prayer

O Lord our God,
we bless you that you chose your first miracle
to be at the wedding-feast at Cana in Galilee,
where a new couple pledged themselves
to each other and to the future of family.

We pray that your blessing
will rest on all those drawn together in love,
on couples who publically commit themselves
to each other before family and witnesses.

Give to all who pledge themselves in marriage,
a shared journey of happiness and peace.
Grant that the hopes and prayers in their hearts
may find fulfilment through your mercy.

When they become troubled or anxious,
when they suffer injury or misfortune,
be for them a comfort and a consolation.

Stay with them until their days are over
and their shared pilgrimage ended.
We pray that you will welcome them
into the everlasting peace of your embrace.

The Proclamation of the Kingdom of God

After John had been arrested, Jesus went into Galilee. There he proclaimed the Good News from God. "The time has come," he said, "and the kingdom of God is close at hand. Repent, and believe the Good News."

Again he began to teach by the lakeside, but such a huge crowd gathered round him that he got into a boat on the lake and sat there. The people were all along the shore, at the water's edge.

He taught them many things in parables, and in the course of his preaching he said to them, "Listen! Imagine a sower going out to sow. Now it happened that, as he sowed, some of the seed fell on the edge of the path, and the birds came and ate it up. Some seed fell on rocky ground where it found little soil and sprang up straightaway, because there was no depth of earth; and when the sun came up it was scorched and, not having any roots, it withered away. Some seed fell into thorns and the thorns grew up and choked it and it produced no crop. And some seeds fell into rich soil and, growing tall and strong, produced crop; and yielded thirty, sixty, even a hundredfold." And he said, "Listen, anyone who has ears to hear!"

(Mark 1:14-15; 4:1-9)

The seed that struggles to grow

At the heart of the Gospel lies Jesus' preaching on the kingdom of God. Throughout his ministry, when Jesus speaks about the kingdom he never defines what it actually is, but offers stories and metaphors that attempt to catch something of what it is like: "The kingdom is like a ... " Thus the parable is the privileged way Jesus uses to speak of different aspects of the kingdom of God.

Among those parables is the sower, in which Jesus reflects on the word that is offered to others and depends on their response. This word is like a seed that is sown by Jesus, a seed that depends on the condition of the ground if it is to grow and bear fruit. Through different types of hearers, the parable explores a variety of responses.

There is the hard-hearted crowd: no matter what they are offered, it is never enough to penetrate their granite exterior. The gift of the Gospel is left abandoned, like litter on the ground. There is the opposite crowd – the enthusiasts – who welcome every novelty that comes, who embrace every fashionable movement. Sadly, they have no depth to them so nothing takes root. Then there is the legion of worriers: although they hear the word, they are always somewhere else in their head, wrestling with their own tragic thinking. These people prefer calamity to words of Good News; they are in love with catastrophe.

Finally, there are the calm people who respect language, those who make space in their life to hear what words mean. These people welcome the word into their heart and make it their own, so that it becomes a part of their very being: when they speak, the new word is a part of their story. The word becomes flesh in them.

These hearers are the model for true Christian discipleship: in giving the word of God a secure place in their heart, their willing collaboration ensures that this word becomes an event in the Christian life. They make words happen. As the poet Emily Dickinson wrote:

A word is dead
When it is said
Some say.
I say
It just begins to live
That day.

The Complete Poems of Emily Dickinson

Today the word of God is still scattered generously, with throwaway style. God still risks his word, hoping we will welcome it and make it our own. Like all seeds, the word of God takes time to grow. The sower knows that he has to wait for the weather, the secret workings of the soil, the slow thrust of life, before he can see the crops emerge. Like the growth of the kingdom of God, it all takes time. If we allow the seed to struggle to grow in us, we will also grow. Eventually the word of God and our own word might become one. That would be a harvest indeed.

Vincent Van Gogh, *The Sower*

Foretaste of lasting glory

Vincent Van Gogh's father and grandfather were both pastors. Vincent tried to follow in their footsteps by teaching Bible classes and preaching, which he did in Isleworth, England. He then studied for the ministry in a seminary near Brussels but failed to be recommended. By 1887 he made a dramatic shift in his life, discovering that he could express his profound love for Christ and those who worked the land through his painting. As he wrote to his brother Theo:

> "I want to do drawings that touch people. I want to progress so far that people will say of my work: he feels deeply; he feels tenderly. What am I in most people's eyes? I am a nobody who has no position is society and never will have. Very well, then, I want my work to show what is in the heart of such a nobody."

Letter #218 (to Theo), July 19-23, 1882

Vincent, who preferred to be known by his first name, had a particular love for the parables and their pictorial power. The motif of a peasant sowing fascinated him and he was fond of Jean-François Millet's treatment, although he thought it lacked colour. In 1888, after settling in Arles in the south of France and two years before his death, he painted a landscape with a sower, dominated by a huge sun, one that acts as a halo for the working farmer.

The blossoming tree that dominates the foreground makes a diagonal division of the canvas, disappearing beyond the frame and opening up a depth of space. The ploughed fields that spread over half the canvas are created with short curving strokes of orange and blue, suggesting they will be a lively beneficiary of the farmer's seeds. The humble, bent figure of the sower, throwing seed on the turned ground, is without any facial definition – perhaps because Vincent saw the sower as himself, hoping that his labour, even at this late stage of the working day, like the message of Christ, might take root in us and flourish.

Prayer

O almighty and loving Father,
whose kingdom is without territory
yet covers all countries of our world,
whose dominion is without borders
yet crosses all frontiers:
we pray that your kingdom will come
and your will be done
on earth as it is in heaven.

Extend your sovereignty
over human hearts and minds,
that all nations might know
the redeeming power of your grace.

Break down hostility and indifference
to the glorious gift of your Son
and the loving Gospel
he shares so generously.

Incline our hearts to hear his Gospel anew,
to welcome it, consenting to the joy of its message.
Hasten the time when our earth
will be filled with the knowledge of your love.

The Transfiguration

Now about eight days after this had been said, he took with him Peter and John and James and went up the mountain to pray. As he prayed, the aspect of his face was changed and his clothing became brilliant as lightning. Suddenly there were two men there talking to him; they were Moses and Elijah appearing in glory, and they were speaking of his passing which he was to accomplish in Jerusalem.

Peter and his companions were heavy with sleep, but they kept awake and saw his glory and the two men standing with him. As these were leaving him, Peter said to Jesus, "Master, it is wonderful for us to be here; so let us make three tents, one for you, one for Moses and one for Elijah." He did not know what he was saying. As he spoke, a cloud came and covered them with shadow; and when they went into the cloud the disciples were afraid.

And a voice came from the cloud saying, "This is my Son, the Chosen One. Listen to him." And after the voice had spoken, Jesus was found alone. The disciples kept silence and, at that time, told no one what they had seen.

(Luke 9:28-36)

The love that transfigures

In the story of the transfiguration we see Jesus become radiant and aglow. As he is identified and affirmed by God as "my Son, the Chosen One", something shows through him that was not evident previously. Jesus has had little success in being recognised by others. The neighbours think they know: "This is Joseph's son, surely." Others think he is Elijah or one of the ancient prophets returned, while others believe he is the devil's agent. Peter says he is the Christ. Nobody gets to the real heart of who Jesus is; soon after he hears all the proposed names he goes up the mountain to pray. With him he takes the inner circle of the apostolic group, Peter, James and John.

In the experience of prayer it is clear that Jesus is not Elijah. Neither is he Moses, the greatest of the ancient prophets. They appear on the scene to direct our attention to a journey Jesus must make to Jerusalem. Peter makes a suggestion that echoes down history: if in doubt, build something. But the focus is not on architectural posterity, but on who Jesus is: "This is my Son, the Chosen One. Listen to him."

Is it any wonder Jesus is radiant and aglow? He has an answer to his prayer. There is someone who gets his name right and that someone is his Father. The deepest part of Jesus is called forth. The Father doesn't just identify Jesus, but affirms him in love as his chosen one, and that transfigures Jesus. That recognition is allied to what Jesus must do: being who he is means he must take the road to Jerusalem.

The transfiguration enables Jesus to make the most difficult journey of his life – to take the road that goes from Galilee to Golgotha.

The Gospel passage tells us that Jesus did not face the knowledge of his forthcoming violent death alone. That lonely knowledge could paralyse anyone. The transfiguration enables Jesus to make that journey to Jerusalem in the declared love of the Father. The direction which Jesus has to follow will cost him his life: Luke shows us that Jesus is not just the one who is to suffer but that he is the beloved Son of God. These two go together.

In our own journeys we can face difficult decisions more surely in the knowledge that we are loved and supported. When we hear our name called in love we can face our own road to Jerusalem. The power of that love funds us to face the future, just as its absence makes the future a loveless landscape. It is that love that we celebrate; it helps us to travel hopefully; it enables us to keep on striving until we can rest at last in the love that best knows our name.

Giovanni Bellini, *The Transfiguration of Christ*

Foretaste of lasting glory

The Venetian master Giovanni Bellini twice painted *The Transfiguration of Christ*, the first around 1460 and the second around 1480. The first version is a more formal painting which was originally commissioned as the central panel of a large altarpiece; it now hangs as a single piece in the Museo Correr, Venice.

We, the viewers, observe, from a respectful distance and from below, this solemn scene. We behold the majesty of Christ flanked by Moses and Elijah, all three standing upright on the crown of the mountain's summit. Immediately below we see the three disciples lying on the rock face, struggling to stay awake. Although the two sets of characters appear physically close, in this scene they inhabit different worlds: Jesus, Moses and Elijah are projected against the backdrop of the heavens, whereas the three disciples slump on the craggy ground of bewilderment and weariness.

Jesus, Moses and Elijah converse about Jesus' final journey which will be accomplished in Jerusalem – a journey not yet undertaken. While Moses, on the left, seems enraptured by the presence of Jesus, the prophet Elijah presses his case, his hands open in sweet reasonableness. The revelation prompts Jesus to hold up his right hand as if in protest. The proposed journey will lead to an appointment with death. After Jesus descends the mountain he leaves his home region of Galilee and "resolutely took the road for Jerusalem" (Luke 9:51).

Lower down, we see the three disciples floundering. His back against the summit, Peter stares up, mystified. James appears lost in sleep. Turning away from the spectacle, young John stares at the nearby sapling, as if this budding tree might help him decode what is going on. Perhaps the sapling does hold the answer. The transfiguration is a momentary revelation of the glory of Christ – one, like the sapling, which heralds greatness yet to come. That greatness will be revealed in the abiding glory of Jesus' resurrection.

Prayer
Heavenly Father,
we bless you for the power and the glory
of your loving presence that transfigured Jesus;
for your words that recognised and affirmed him
as your Beloved Son, your Chosen One.

May his courage and steadfast loyalty,
his unswerving devotion to do your will,
inspire and strengthen all of us
to follow the road which love bids us take,
even when it leads through darkness and suffering.

Keep us, Father, ever mindful and grateful
of your boundless and generous love
which enabled Jesus to face Jerusalem
and empowers us to face the future with confidence
in the sure knowledge of your safe keeping.

Guide and protect us here on earth
that we may enjoy eternal rest
when our journey is finished
and our work is done.

The Institution of the Eucharist

When the hour came, he took his place at table, and the apostles with him. And he said to them, "I have longed to eat this Passover with you before I suffer; because I tell you, I shall not eat it again until it is fulfilled in the kingdom of God."

Then taking a cup, he gave thanks and said, "Take this and share it among you, because from now on, I tell you, I shall not drink wine until the kingdom of God comes."

Then he took some bread and when he had given thanks, broke it and gave it to them saying, "This is my body which will be given for you; do this as a memorial of me." He did the same with the cup after supper and said, "This cup is the new covenant in my blood which will be poured out for you.

And yet here with me on the table is the hand of the man who betrays me. The Son of Man does indeed go to his fate even as it has been decreed, but alas for that man by whom he is betrayed!" And they began to ask one another which of them it could be who was to do this thing.

A dispute arose also between them about which should be reckoned the greatest, but he said to them, "Among pagans it is the kings who lord it over them, and those who have authority over them are given the title Benefactor. This must not happen with you. No; the greatest among you must behave as if he were the youngest, the leader as if he were the one who serves. For who is the greater: the one at table or the one who serves? The one at table, surely. Yet here am I among you as one who serves!"

(Luke 22:14-27)

The greatest gift

Jesus has longed to share this final meal with his disciples. Before he is handed over to his enemies, Jesus hands himself over, with care, to his friends. He puts himself into their safekeeping, our safekeeping. He takes the bread and solemnly says: "This is my body which will be given for you; do this as a memorial of me." It is a body given, pledged, bequeathed. Jesus hands over his body – not his ideas or his insights or his teachings – as his final gift to his friends. There is nothing more personal than this, his greatest gift. What more could he give?

But when we look at the whole setting of the Last Supper we see a mixture of things going on: we know there is disloyalty in the room and it does not all belong to the company treasurer; there is awkwardness and confusion, ambition and avoidance. That atmosphere of cross-talk and distraction are present at this most solemn moment. Jesus will finish this meal by protesting to his disciples: "That is enough!" (Luke 22:38) and will then set out for a garden of grief.

Just as the apostles were preoccupied and anxious at the Last Supper, that same drama can be repeated at our own Eucharists. Who knows what people carry in their hearts as they pass the holy water font? Who knows what haunts them or what hurts them?

But the good news is that Jesus can live with that ambiguity. At the Last Supper Jesus was not breaking bread for a council of warriors, but for his own fragile followers whom he loved. The Eucharist is always bread broken for broken people. Jesus keeps telling us that our vulnerable humanity does not have to be denied or disguised to be accepted; rather in its fragility, in its shaky beauty, it is uplifted and transformed in the love of Christ.

That night before his death, Jesus said his words of goodbye: "Do this as a memorial of me." When I am gone, remember me by doing this. Gather together, tell the story, break the bread and share this blessed experience with others.

This action has been done in Gothic cathedrals and mud huts, in great amphitheatres and on battlefields, before kings and peasants; and it will continue to be done until the end of time.

As the *Catechism of the Catholic Church* states:

> "It is highly fitting that Christ should have wanted to remain present to his Church in this unique way. Since Christ was about to take his departure from his own in his visible form, he wanted to give us his sacramental presence; since he was about to offer himself on the cross to save us, he wanted us to have the memorial of the love which he loved us 'to the end', even to the giving of his life. In his Eucharistic presence he remains mysteriously in our midst as the one who loved us and gave himself up for us." (1380)

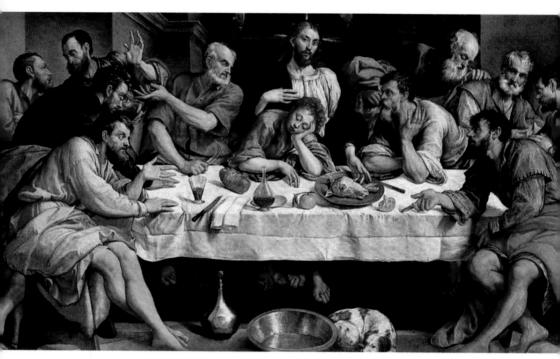

Jacopo Bassano, *The Last Supper*

Bread broken for broken people

Jacopo dal Ponte was so attached to his own town of Bassano, some forty miles northwest of Venice, that he changed his name to Jacopo Bassano. He was trained by his father, Francesco, and later set up his own workshop in the town, establishing a family practice which was eventually serviced by his four sons. Most of his work consists of biblical themes with an intense attention to naturalistic details, always with a sympathetic eye to domestic settings and animals. Here, in *The Last Supper*, painted in 1542, he has a small dog lying contentedly at the feet of Jesus. Not forgetting the watchful cat…

Unlike Da Vinci's beautifully ordered *Last Supper* with Jesus and the apostles sitting in a neat row behind a long table, Bassano's painting has them crowding round a table too small to accommodate all of them. Bassano catches in exquisite detail the fragility of this company. None of the apostles is paying any attention to Jesus: no eyes are fixed on him; no ears attentive to what he might be struggling to say. This is a concelebration of distraction.

The apostles prefer to address their own concern, fretful about their place in the scheme of things: which of them is the greatest? Their worry about hierarchy overshadows Jesus' talk of his approaching death. The Beloved Disciple, immediately in front of Jesus, absents himself from the apostolic seminar; Judas, on the upper right of the painting, remains withdrawn, having his own deadly appointment to keep.

In the midst of all this distraction, Jesus looks out at us, the onlooker, while pointing out the head of the slaughtered lamb on a dish. He hopes that we might attend him and appreciate a simple truth: in spite of the muddle of life surrounding us, he offers us himself, real food. Clearly, as Bassano knew, it is bread broken for broken people.

Prayer

Lord Jesus Christ,
who emptied yourself of all glory
and came among us as one who served:
we thank you for your greatest gift
in giving your blessed body to us
as a memorial of your love.

Deliver us from pride and false ambition;
may we never despise or deride
our brothers and sisters.
Let us follow your example
of heroic and generous love.

Give us the true courage
that shows itself in gentleness;
the true wisdom
that shows itself in simplicity;
the true authority
that shows itself in decency.

And may your blessing
always accompany us.

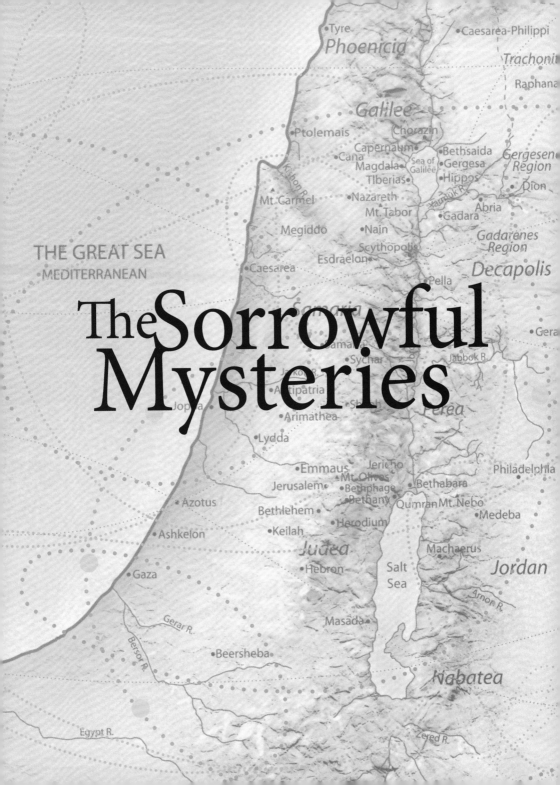

The Sorrowful Mysteries

The Agony in the Garden

The Scourging at the Pillar

The Crowning with Thorns

The Carrying of the Cross

The Crucifixion

The Agony in the Garden

They came to a small estate called Gethsemane, and Jesus said to his disciples, "Stay here while I pray." Then he took Peter and James and John with him. And a sudden fear came over him, and great distress. And he said to them, "My soul is sorrowful to the point of death. Wait, here and keep awake."

And going on a little further he threw himself on the ground and prayed that, if it were possible, this hour might pass him by. "Abba, (Father)!" he said. "Everything is possible for you. Take the cup away from me. But let it be as you, not I, would have it."

He came back and found them sleeping, and he said to Peter, "Simon, are you asleep? Had you not the strength to keep awake for one hour? You should be awake, and praying not to be put to the test. The spirit is willing, but the flesh is weak." Again he went away and prayed, saying the same words.

And once more he came back and found them sleeping, their eyes were so heavy; and they could find no answer for him.

He came back a third time and said to them, "You can sleep on now and take your rest. It is all over. The hour has come. Now the Son of Man is to be betrayed into the hands of sinners. Get up! Let us go! My betrayer is close at hand already."

(Mark 14:32-42)

Waiting and praying

The scene in Gethsemane begins with Jesus and the disciples entering the olive grove together. It ends with Jesus being arrested and led away while the disciples abandon him. Jesus distances himself from the two groups of disciples, goes apart by himself, throws himself on the ground and awaits an answer to his prayer: "Abba, Father, all things are possible for you. Take this cup away. But let it be as you, not I, will it." Jesus prays to discover the will of his Father, promising that when he discovers what it is, he will do it.

Geographically, Gethsemane is well placed for escape: Jesus could turn his back on the city of Jerusalem and the Kidron Valley, climb the Mount of Olives in fifteen minutes, and head into the Judean wilderness which lies immediately east. No arresting party would follow him into the wilderness at night.

Hoping to avoid the torment of staying in place and facing the time ahead, Jesus implores his Father to spare him. He beseeches his disciples to help him find an answer to his predicament. But, as Mark notes in his telling phrase, "they could find no answer for him." The sleep of the disciples is not surprising: while it is difficult to wait with those who suffer and pay attention to their plight, it is even more demanding when that person is your fearful leader.

For most people, leadership and vulnerability do not sit easily together. We expect our leaders to be in control, exuding authority and power: we do not expect to see them lying on the ground begging God to free them from what is to come and asking us for help. Is it any wonder that the disciples turn away from this scene?

Jesus is waiting for the time of terror to begin. People who have survived torture tell us that the time of waiting is one of absolute dread: you become unnerved and everything is thrown into doubt – your own identity, your own sense of purpose, your own capacity to survive and hold on to what you believe. Yet Jesus eventually turns away from thoughts of escape and turns towards consent. Through his prayer, Jesus comes to a decision to endure the trial ahead. In that decision, Jesus reckons that his suffering will be overcome only if accepted; that the feeling of being abandoned by God will be conquered only if endured; that the experience of rejection will be transformed only if embraced.

Gethsemane is an image of sorrowful waiting; of being present to the prospect of what people will do to you; of suffering the consequences of other people's decisions; of becoming an object in their hands. Half of the world lives in Gethsemane and the other half is asleep.

But Gethsemane is also a story of resolve: to abide by whatever you settled for in life; to stay steadfast to your calling in the face of brutal opposition. Gethsemane, for Jesus, is a crucial decision: he chooses to honour his ancient appointment with death. Before Judas hands over Jesus to the Temple authorities, Jesus hands himself over to the will of his Father.

Giovanni Bellini, *The Agony in the Garden*

Resolution in the garden

Following his teacher and brother-in-law, Andrea Mantegna, Bellini painted the dramatic account of Jesus' agony in the garden: both paintings hang next to each other in the National Gallery, London. Painted around 1465, Bellini's scene does not take place in the dead of night. Instead, it is lit with sunrise which illuminates the whole setting, giving it a three-dimensional quality. The undersides of the grey clouds are orange; the hilltop town is bathed in dawn light; the darkness of the night is being dismissed from the nearby hills. Bellini's light infuses this anxious scene with new hope.

Jesus, awake and alert, is kneeling on a rocky outcrop, his praying hands resting on top of the rock that appears not unlike an altar. The cup – the symbol of approaching sacrifice that Jesus begged God to take away – is held out to him by an angel: Bellini's cup is now a chalice with a covering paten, lit by the rising sun. These two objects are central in the Mass: the paten which holds the body of Christ and the cup which holds the blood of Christ. The angel is not displaying them; his outstretched arms indicate that he is offering them to Jesus. This is the moment for decision and resolution.

In the mid-background the arresting party, brandishing their weapons and led by Judas, now have Jesus within sight. As they approach the flowing brook of the Kidron Valley, they will surely arrive at their destination within minutes. In the foreground the three sleeping disciples are unaware of the drama going on around them: Peter lies on his back on the rock face; James sleeps, his left arm serving as a pillow; John leans against an outcrop of bizarre rock. We notice that they sleep between the dead tree on the left and the broken-down guard rail on the right.

Bellini manages, with great delicacy, to capture the beauty of an otherwise tragic scene: the moment Jesus fully accepts his saving mission – a new dawn indeed.

Prayer

Lord Jesus Christ,
who emptied yourself of all glory
and came among us as one who serves:
we thank you for your greatest gift
in giving your blessed body to us
as a memorial of your love.

Deliver us from pride and false ambition;
may we never despise or deride
our brothers and sisters.
Let us follow your example
of heroic and generous love.

Give us the true courage
that shows itself in gentleness;
the true wisdom
that shows itself in simplicity;
the true authority
that shows itself in decency.

And may your blessing
always accompany us.

The Scourging at the Pillar

At festival time Pilate used to release a prisoner for them, anyone they asked for. Now a man called Barabbas was then in prison with the rioters who had committed murder during the uprising. When the crowd went up and began to ask Pilate the customary favour, Pilate answered them, "Do you want me to release for you the king of the Jews?" For he realised it was out of jealousy that the chief priests had handed Jesus over. The chief priests, however, had incited the crowd to demand that he should release Barabbas for them instead.

Then Pilate spoke again. "But in that case," he said to them, "what am I to do with the man you call the king of the Jews?" They shouted back, "Crucify him!" "Why?" Pilate asked them. "What harm has he done?" But they shouted all the louder, "Crucify him!"

So Pilate, anxious to placate the crowd, released Barabbas for them and, having ordered Jesus to be scourged, handed him over to be crucified.

(Mark 15:6-15)

To survive in power

Pilate comes to Jerusalem with his auxiliary troops only for the major Jewish festivals, to keep order in the overcrowded city swarming with pilgrims; otherwise he lives in the coastal capital of Caesarea. The release of a prisoner at the principal Jewish festival of Passover is not tender-heartedness on the part of the Roman governor: it is an astute political decision to curry the favour of the leaders and the crowd, thus hopefully avoiding disturbance throughout the city. Passover is the most dangerous date in Pilate's calendar and his goal is to keep the peace, Pax Romana, curbing any high-risk threat that might reflect badly on his own authority.

Pilate, aware that Jesus commands no troops and poses no threat to Rome, knows that it is out of jealousy that the chief priests want Jesus executed. He is not going to risk the wrath of the religious leaders and the crowd; he has no interest in ensuring justice for Jesus if the outcome is a riot. Pilate forces the crowd to make a decision. For him, the advantage of the Passover pardon is that the Jewish chief priests, not the Roman governor, can take responsibility for the death of Jesus. He releases Jesus Bar Abba (Barabbas) and hands Jesus of Nazareth over to the torturers to be whipped and then crucified.

When Paul wants to commend himself to the Christian community in Corinth he writes: "Five times I had the thirty-nine lashes from the Jews; three times I have been beaten by sticks" (2 Corinthians 11:24). The Jewish tradition set a limit of forty lashes, the practice being to stop at thirty-nine to ensure staying within the limits of the Law. The Romans set no such limitation. Flagellation was a common punishment which judges inflicted on offenders, usually criminals, slaves and foreigners. In a Roman court of law neither flagellation nor crucifixion was imposed on Roman citizens except for high treason.

The instruments of torture consisted of whips, scourges and leather straps. There were whips made from bared twigs (willow, birch or hazel); there were cords made from twisted parchment; there was the plain leather strap; the most severe was a thong made from ox-leather, supplemented with lead weights or nails or small hard bones. The choice of instrument and the number of lashes were left to the judge.

None of the Gospels dwells on the scene of Jesus being scourged: there is no description of which instruments are used, how many torturers are involved, how many lashes are given, how long the punishment lasts or how Jesus manages to endure it. The Gospels are not just spare in their description but wholly silent. We are left to guess the suffering that Jesus experienced and the wounds he sustained.

We are also left to guess the sufferings of thousands of people in today's world, whose innocence is abused because a desperate leader is determined to avoid being toppled from power. The story continues.

Caravaggio, *The Flagellation of Christ*

Torture in secret

Caravaggio, the name by which Michelangelo Merisi came to be known, was his family's home town, some forty kilometres east of Milan. In 1557, when Caravaggio was six, the bubonic plague hit the region and he lost most of his family, including his father and grandfather. His mother survived until Caravaggio was eleven. Then the orphan took to the streets with a local gang until he won an apprenticeship in Milan, which he served until his late teens. That traumatic childhood was to haunt the painter for the rest of his life.

Moving to Rome, he established himself quickly as a brilliant artist but had to flee the city after murdering a rival. He escaped to Naples, where he painted *The Flagellation of Christ*. Caravaggio has taken this Gospel event out of the public forum and placed it in a dark interior space, like a cavernous dungeon. No one witnesses this brutal ballet except us, the privileged viewers. We are drawn into its chilling realism, directed by Caravaggio's use of light, accentuating the unmarked body of Jesus as the torturers prepare for their barbaric sport.

The man on the right is tying Jesus to the column while at the same time kicking on Jesus' right calf, forcing the body of Jesus to stumble forwards as his legs twist sharply, bending at the knees. On the left we see the scowling features of this torturer's face as he grabs a fistful of the victim's hair with his left hand. With flay at the ready in his right hand, he stiffens his arm for the first lash. The third torturer stoops to prepare another weapon as he ropes the branches together, his profile silhouetted against Jesus' thigh.

Like most tortures, this one is carried out in secret: it will begin presently. For the moment we behold the immaculate body of the innocent one, radiant in full light, surrounded by darkness and brutality.

Prayer

We bless you, dear Lord,
for enduring the violence
of your scourging at the pillar
and the heartless abuse
meted out by your torturers.

When we are in the dark of suffering,
shed your gracious light upon us.
When we are struck by misfortune,
console us with your loving presence.
When our flesh is weak and overburdened,
strengthen our resolve to persevere.
When we feel utterly alone,
assure us of your loving attendance.

We pray for all innocent people
who are tortured in secret
throughout our broken world.
Be with them in their fear and loneliness,
in the agony of their diminishment
and in the face of execution and death.

Forgive all injustice in our lives,
and transform us to act
as instruments of your peace.

It is by your wounds that we are healed.

The Crowning with Thorns

Pilate then had Jesus taken away and scourged; and after this, the soldiers twisted some thorns into a crown and put it on his head, and dressed him in a purple robe. They kept coming up to him and saying, "Hail, king of the Jews!" and they slapped him in the face.

Pilate came outside again and said to them, "Look, I am going to bring him out to you to let you see that I find no case." Jesus then came out wearing the crown of thorns and the purple robe. Pilate said, "Here is the man." When they saw him the chief priests and the guards shouted, "Crucify him! Crucify him!" Pilate said, "Take him yourselves and crucify him: I can find no case against him." "We have a Law," the Jews replied, "and according to that Law he ought to die, because he has claimed to be the Son of God."

(John 19:1-7)

Now as Pilate was seated on the chair of judgement, his wife sent him a message, "Have nothing to do with that man; I have been upset all day by a dream I had about him."

(Matthew 27:19)

Real power

An indecisive and nervous Roman governor orders Jesus to be taken away and scourged. Perhaps Pilate hopes that this will placate the determined religious leaders and their rented crowd, thus releasing him from further hassle. If the opposition views the prisoner badly disfigured, bent, broken and bleeding, they might revise their estimate of the imagined threat they believe he poses.

After brutal punishment, how could this shattered human being, this wrecked northerner from the hills of Galilee, pose a threat to the sober religious establishment of the city of Jerusalem? What is it, anyway, about this Jesus who seems to have such an easy gift for making religious leaders nervous? Not just religious leaders, it has to be said.

The governor's soldiers do more than their superior commands them. Spending most of their life confined to quarters, forever waiting for conflict and disturbance to prove themselves, they flesh out this order for their own entertainment. They decide to humiliate the prisoner, not just punish him, dressing him up as a king in the purple reserved for their emperor. They crown him, not with laurel leaves, but with angry thorns.

This gives them the opportunity, not only of mocking the prisoner, but also the authority they serve, one that uses them blithely, every day, for its own purpose. They slap the face of Jesus and everything they are compelled to serve. And in the midst of this spectacle, there is no reported reaction from Jesus. He is silent.

As Seamus Heaney observed in his poem, *Weighing In*:

> Prophesy who struck thee! When soldiers mocked
> Blindfolded Jesus and he didn't strike back
> They were neither shamed nor edified, although
> Something was made manifest – the power
> Of power not exercised, of hope inferred
> By the powerless forever.

Seamus Heaney, The Spirit Level

That curious power, that of power not exercised, is one that silently dominates this scene when two other forceful competitors, civil and religious, challenge one another.

In all the mighty conflicts that dominate our world, sometimes it is the victim who radiates real power, a power that awaits its destined time.

Antonio Ciseri, *Ecce Homo*

A woman's protest

Antonio Ciseri, a Swiss-Italian artist, painted *Ecce Homo* in 1871; it now hangs in the Galleria d'Arte Moderna in Florence. Ciseri spent most of his life in Florence, where he ran a school of art while also working on a series of commissions mostly for religious painting and portraiture.

This painting looks like a still from a film set: the action is paused. From the balcony of his palace in the upper city of Jerusalem, we see Pilate, surrounded by his Praetorian Guard and advisers. He puts Jesus on display to the angry crowd: Ecce Homo – Behold the Man. His transparent white toga reflects the carved limestone of the surrounding buildings. Pressing his argument, the governor leans over the balcony as he pleads with the crowd below; his left hand, thumb upraised, gestures towards the one he believes has no case to answer.

We have the advantage of viewing this scene from the cool marble interior of the Herodian palace as we look out at the protesting crowd in the bright Mediterranean sunshine. We see Jesus with eyes downcast, standing erect and looking remarkably dignified in spite of the uproar below and above him. Handcuffed and crowned with thorns, Jesus wears a scarlet robe which has now slipped off his shoulders; he stands calmly facing the crowd that clamours for his death. His upper body is unmarked with no visible signs of wounds; he exudes all the dignity of a king.

The only face we can properly see is that of Pilate's wife. She has just warned her husband to have nothing to do with Jesus. Now that he is debating Jesus' fate with the crowds rather than pronouncing his final judgement, she turns her back on him, resting an arm on the shoulder of her handmaid, admitting defeat. She leaves crestfallen, no doubt guessing that her nightmares will only intensify.

Among this vast religious crowd, mostly male, this Gentile woman is the one closest to Jesus.

Prayer

Lord Jesus Christ, holy and merciful one,
you suffered in silence
when you were made the object
of the soldiers' brutal attention;
you were dressed up as a king
with a crown of thorns pressed on your head;
you were tormented and derided,
then paraded as a spectacle
for the entertainment of the mob.

You did not meet violence with violence
but endured what was done to you.
Help us always to reverence
your way, your truth and your forbearance.
Keep us always mindful of your boundless love.

Take from us all bitterness and resentment
towards our fellow human beings;
make us agents of your compassion
to the suffering, the persecuted
and all who are oppressed by violence.
Grace us always with your strength and solace.

The Carrying of the Cross

As they were leading him away they seized on a man, Simon from Cyrene, who was coming in from the country, and made him shoulder the cross and carry it behind Jesus. Large numbers of people followed him, and of women too, who mourned and lamented for him.

But Jesus turned to them and said, "Daughters of Jerusalem, do not weep for me; weep rather for yourselves and for your children. For the days will surely come when people will say, 'Happy are those who are barren, the wombs that have never borne, the breasts that have never suckled!' Then they will begin to say to the mountains, 'Fall on us!'; to the hills, 'Cover us!' For if men use the green wood like this, what will happen when it is dry?"

Now with him they were also leading out two other criminals to be executed.

(Luke 23:26-32)

The way of the cross

After being condemned to death Jesus is led away to the place of execution, making his final journey, the infamous way of the cross. Pilate's Praetorium, his place of judgement, was either at the Antonia fortress beside the Temple or the Herodian palace in the upper city, where the governor resided during his stay in Jerusalem. In either case the way to Golgotha is not a long journey.

For the Romans, the usual place of crucifixion was outside the main city gates, making their authority highly visible and acting as a gruesome warning to any locals or visitors of the finality of Roman justice. If you rule by terror, you ensure the terror is visible and felt.

There were a number of upright stakes permanently fixed along the road – fixed because they were used regularly. The condemned man would carry the cross-beam or *patibulum* on his shoulders, his hands roped to the wood, while around his neck he would carry the charge or *titulus* made against him. On arrival at the crucifixion site the criminal was nailed or roped to the cross-beam and the charge against him was nailed above his head for everyone to see. The cross-beam was then raised and slotted into a groove on top of the stake.

Jesus makes his way to the killing fields but he is growing ever weaker. A passing stranger, Simon of Cyrene, is compelled to help Jesus carry the cross. This arrangement is not a sign of unexpected compassion from the authorities: they want to avoid the victim dying on the way to crucifixion. Earlier Jesus announced to the crowds: "Anyone who does not carry his cross and come after me cannot be my disciple" (Luke 14:27). Now that his chosen disciples have gone their own way, Simon is now the model of true discipleship.

The women of Jerusalem openly lament Jesus' suffering and shame. He tells them, however, that they have better cause to weep for themselves because of the fate which awaits the inhabitants of Jerusalem. Jesus predicts the city's destruction and warns that the Romans will inflict such debasement and destruction on them that they will beg the mountains to fall on them and bury them. Jesus says: "For if men use the green wood like this, what will happen when it is dry?" In other words: if Jesus' innocence is abused and assaulted so severely, what will happen to those who are guilty?

Even on the way of the cross Jesus reaches out in compassion, warning the women that a worse fate awaits them and their families when the Romans will surely come to destroy their city. Rather than focusing on his own fate, he sympathises with theirs, which will be even more horrific. In the midst of his own suffering, Jesus maintains his particular love for the last and the least: these brave women, who are the only ones to show any sympathy on this lonely way of the cross.

Where was everyone else? Where were all the sick people he healed? The sinners he forgave? The crowds he fed? Those possessed he released? Where were all the disciples he called to follow him? Why so few?

Hieronymus Bosch, *Christ Carrying the Cross*

Serenity amidst brutality

Born around 1450 in the duchy of Brabant (now in the Netherlands), Hieronymus Bosch came from a family of artists. A committed Catholic, Bosch joined the Brotherhood of Our Lady, a local religious fraternity. Towards the end of the fifteenth century there was a growing appetite for images of the suffering Christ, many for private devotional use. Bosch received his first commissions on this theme from the Brotherhood. He was fascinated by the duality of good and evil: in many of his paintings he depicts the cruel misery of people's lives forever surrounded by demonic forces.

Against a dark background, Bosch depicts Jesus carrying the cross in the midst of a tangle of heads, mostly caricatures of humanity with grotesque features. Finished in 1515, the work now hangs in the Museum of Fine Arts in Ghent. The painting has a total of eighteen portraits – nineteen if you include the impression on Veronica's veil. She is situated on the lower left, showing us an image of Jesus more perfect than any artist could render it; her face is lit from the holy reflection. In the lower right corner, three tormentors, one wearing a magician's hat, taunt the impenitent thief: he looks unfazed by their browbeating.

On the upper right of the painting there is the good thief being hectored by an ugly, monkish figure on the right and an ear-ringed elder on the left. Christ's torturers were popularly referred to as savage dogs and, to the right of Jesus, we see a man with chains on his face, teeth bared, howling. The upper left of the painting is reserved for Simon of Cyrene. With upturned face and outstretched arms, he tries to ease the weight of the cross from Jesus' shoulders.

And in the midst of this brutal theatre there is the serene Jesus, eyes closed as if drawing strength from a secret sanctuary within. Jesus carries on. Stubborn love, as we all know, often makes its way with a cross on its back.

Prayer

O holy and loving Redeemer,
by whose wounds we are healed,
by whose cross we are liberated:
when we are called to bear your cross
like Simon of Cyrene of old,
let us rejoice in this privilege
and endure it for your sake.

Be for us our companion on the way,
a support in our weariness,
a shielding in danger,
a shelter in the storm,
a shade in the heat,
an assurance in disappointment.

The Via Dolorosa winds its way
through all the towns and villages in our land,
through every home, past every door.
Help us, dear Lord, to attend with mercy
those who walk their way of the cross:
those who are struck down by misfortune;
those who are afflicted by violence;
those who are abused and oppressed.

Be their light and their guide
this day and always.

The Crucifixion

They then took charge of Jesus and, carrying his own cross, he went out of the city to the place of the skull or, as it was called in Hebrew, Golgotha, where they crucified him with two others, one on either side with Jesus in the middle. Pilate wrote out a notice and had it fixed to the cross; it ran: "Jesus the Nazarene, King of the Jews". This notice was read by many of the Jews, because the place where Jesus was crucified was not far from the city and the writing was in Hebrew, Latin and Greek. So the Jewish chief priests said to Pilate, "You should not write 'King of the Jews', but, 'this man said: I am King of the Jews'." Pilate answered, "What I have written, I have written."

When the soldiers had finished crucifying Jesus they took his clothing and divided it into four shares, one for each soldier. His undergarment was seamless, woven in one piece from neck to hem; so they said to one another, "Instead of tearing it, let's throw dice to decide who is to have it." In this way the words of scripture were fulfilled:

> They shared out my clothing among them,
> They cast lots for my clothes.

This is exactly what the soldiers did. Near the cross of Jesus stood his mother and his mother's sister, Mary the wife of Cleopas, and Mary of Magdala. Seeing his mother and the disciple he loved standing near her, Jesus said to his mother, "Woman this is your son." Then to the disciple he said, "This is your mother." And from that moment the disciple made a place for her in his home.

After this, Jesus knew that everything had now been completed, and to fulfil the scripture perfectly he said:

> "I am thirsty."

A jar full of vinegar stood there, so putting a sponge soaked in the vinegar on a hyssop stick they held it up to his mouth. After Jesus had taken the vinegar he said, "It is accomplished"; and bowing his head he gave up his spirit.

(John 19:17-30)

"It is accomplished"

More space is devoted to the argument between Pilate and the chief priests about the charge against Jesus than to the actual death of Jesus. Sometimes in life, as in death, marginal problems assume sudden and senseless importance. While someone is dying, others argue about trivial issues: in the meantime the real drama unfolds and you might wonder who is paying attention.

Like the other evangelists, John's language is spare and restrained when describing Jesus' death. The charge against Jesus forms the only words we know were written about Jesus during his lifetime. This was fixed to the cross for everyone to see. The legal proclamation is written in three languages: Hebrew, the traditional language of the Jews; Latin, the official language of Roman government; Greek, the spoken language of the eastern Roman Empire. In many paintings and sculptures this is shortened to four letters, INRI – *Jesus Nazarenus Rex Judaeorum* – Jesus of Nazareth King of the Jews. While the Jewish chief priests protest against Pilate's wording, the governor proves unyielding, no doubt pleased he has succeeded in antagonising these troublesome leaders.

In his crucifixion scene, the evangelist John has the three Marys and the Beloved Disciple standing at the foot of the cross. Mary, the mother of Jesus, represents the family of Jesus; the Beloved Disciple represents his disciples. In this tender setting, we watch Jesus reach out beyond his own torment to speak his last will and testament, bringing his family and his disciples together. Jesus uses his dying moments to ensure that the two people he loves most – his mother and his Beloved Disciple –

will become one caring family. He leaves behind him the beginnings of a new, loving community.

You remember that, at the wedding feast of Cana, Jesus responded to the shortage of wine by turning the water in six stone jars into the finest wine. Now, facing death, Jesus expresses his thirst and he is given vinegar – the lowest grade of sour wine used by common soldiers. At Cana he told his mother that his hour had not yet come. Now, on the cross, his hour is upon him and he is able in his final words to celebrate its completion. With great dignity Jesus says, "It is accomplished."

The death of Jesus is not some catastrophic mishap devoid of meaning, but the fulfilment of a life's purpose, the proof of love's endeavour and the completion of a chronicle of salvation:

> Yes, God loved the world so much
> that he gave his only Son,
> so that everyone who believes in him may not be lost
> but may have eternal life.
> For God sent his Son into the world
> not to condemn the world,
> but so that through him the world might be saved.
> (John 3:16-17)

In the midst of all this suffering something extraordinary is being disclosed: the love of God is revealed at its most telling in the most vulnerable moment in Jesus' life – his dying.

Matthias Grünewald, *The Crucifixion*

Unsparing savagery

There is no painting in the history of religious art that portrays the brutality of crucifixion and the suffering of Christ like Matthias Grünewald's central panel of this famous altarpiece. What the four evangelists pass over in discreet silence – the wretched torment of Jesus – Grünewald puts on stage without discretion or delicacy. This is raw, intense and unapologetic.

The Isenheim Altarpiece was commissioned by the abbot of a monastic community in Isenheim, specialising in caring for patients suffering from skin diseases. Today this work is displayed in the Musée Colmar in Alsace. Constructed and painted between 1512 and 1516, the enormous moveable altarpiece formed the central object of devotion in the hospital chapel.

Against an eerie barren landscape, the gruesome figure of the dying Christ hangs from the crossbeam, bending from his weight. We see his skin swollen and torn as a result of the flagellation – a powerful image in a hospital that specialised in skin complaints. The blood from his side runs down into his ripped loincloth. His claw-like fingers clutch at the air. His head, spiked with thorns, collapses to the right.

The mother of Jesus, dressed in dazzling white, faints into the waiting arms of the Beloved Disciple. As she loses the only fruit of her womb, she falls in to the arms of her new son. Mary of Magdala kneels before the cross, wringing her hands in sorrow, her agonised fingers echoing those of Christ. Her jar of ointment awaits its sacred task. On the other side stands the powerful figure of John the Baptist; at John's feet is the Lamb of God, holding the cross and bleeding into a chalice. The Latin inscription behind John reads "He must grow greater: I must grow smaller" (John 3:30) – a truth which Grünewald illustrates by presenting the body of Jesus significantly larger than the four attendant figures.

This German artist is unmoved by the figurative beauty and majesty of the Italian Renaissance: he elects to depict the long dark night of the soul with graphic and savage insistence. This is the price paid for such enduring love.

Prayer

Beloved Lord Jesus Christ,
who endured the shame and bitterness
of the way of the cross and the crucifixion,
yet reached out beyond your suffering
to unite your family and followers:
kindle in our hearts gratitude
for the love that moves beyond its own pain,
for the kindness that attends the distress of others,
for the forgiveness that releases from bondage.

Grant that we may never presume on your mercy,
but live as people who have been forgiven much.
Help us never to nurse anger or hoard hurt;
make us tender and compassionate towards others
that you might forgive us
as we forgive those who sin against us.

Preserve, dear Lord, in love, all those
to whom we are bound by ties of family and affection;
refresh our homes with your abiding presence
and sanctify all our human relationships.
We pray that in the hour of our own trial,
when we are covered in darkness,
we may be strengthened by your kindly light.

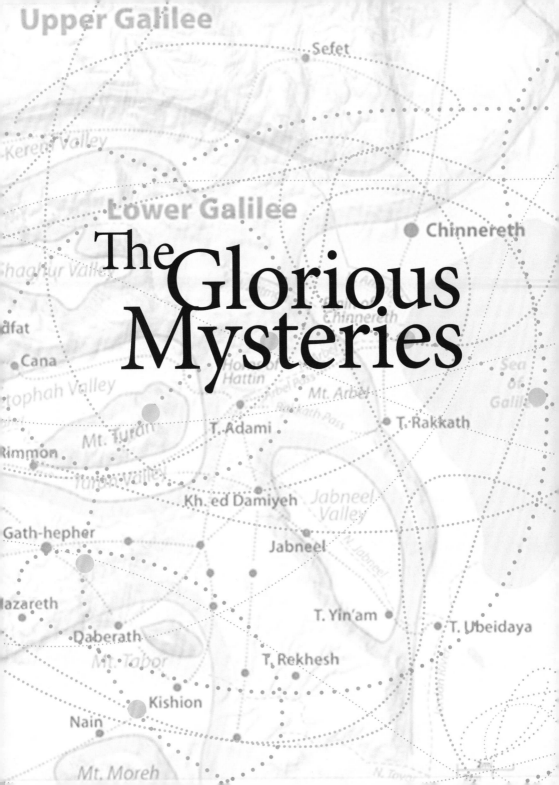

The Glorious Mysteries

The Resurrection

The Ascension

The Descent of the Holy Spirit

The Assumption of the Blessed Virgin into Heaven

The Coronation of the Blessed Virgin Mary

The Resurrection

That very same day, two of them were on their way to a village called
Emmaus, seven miles from Jerusalem, and they were talking together about
all that had happened. Now as they talked this over, Jesus himself came up
and walked by their side; but something prevented them from recognising
him. He said to them, "What matters are you discussing as you walk along?"
They stopped short, their faces downcast.

Then one of them, called Cleopas, answered him, "You must be the only
person staying in Jerusalem who does not know the things that have been
happening there these last few days." "What things?" he asked. "All about
Jesus of Nazareth," they answered, "who proved he was a great prophet by
the things he said and did in the sight of God and of the whole people; and
how our chief priests and our leaders handed him over to be sentenced to
death, and had him crucified. Our own hope had been that he would be the
one to set Israel free…"

Then he said to them, "You foolish men! So slow to believe the full message
of the prophets! Was it not ordained that the Christ should suffer and so enter
into his glory?" Then starting with Moses and going through all the prophets,
he explained to them the passages of scripture that were about himself.

When they drew near to the village to which they were going, he made as
if to go on; but they pressed him to stay with them. "It is nearly evening,"
they said, "and the day is almost over." So he went in to stay with them. Now
while he was with them at table, he took the bread and said the blessing;
then he broke it and handed it to them. And their eyes were opened and
they recognised him; but he vanished from their sight. Then they said to one
another, "Did our hearts not burn within us as he talked to us on the road and
explained the scriptures to us?"

They set out that instant and returned to Jerusalem. There they found the
Eleven assembled together with their companions, who said to them, "Yes,
it is true. The Lord has risen and has appeared to Simon." Then they told their
story of what had happened on the road and how they had recognised him at
the breaking of bread.

(Luke 24:13-21, 25-35)

Making sense of Jesus' death

None of the Gospels describes the actual resurrection of Jesus: each passes over the event in total silence, acknowledging that God's eternal act is beyond the range of narrative expression. The Gospels move on to show how Jesus' resurrection affects his followers. On the first Easter Sunday we watch two disciples struggling to make sense of the recent death of Jesus. They leave Jerusalem behind them as the place where their hopes met with final defeat. During their walking wake they discuss everything that has happened. When a stranger joins them on the road, they share the story of their hurt and disappointment: Jesus, the one they had hoped would set Israel free, has now been put to death.

The two disciples cannot understand how the death of Jesus can be understood as anything more than a tragic end to a promising life. So the disciples mourn not only the death of Jesus but also the death of their relationship with him. Who are they now? Now they are ex-disciples of a dead prophet with nowhere to go but away. Their cherished hope is now but a memory. The lines that Lord Byron wrote in 1814 could apply to them:

> And all that Memory loves the most
> Was once our only Hope to be:
> And all that Hope adored and lost
> Hath melted into Memory.

The Complete Works of Lord Byron Vol II

Only when they have finished their own story does the stranger begin his own. He invites them to look at the past again, this time in the light of scripture. He offers a wholly different interpretation of the same event as he sees the death of Christ as something which was essential for his glory.

As the stranger helps the two disciples to make sense of the past in a new light, they respond by inviting him to stay with them. When they go in to table they break bread together. The stranger gives himself away by giving himself away to them, in the bread. He is the risen Jesus, and he leaves them with hearts that burn and with eyes that see. Not only does he help them to reinterpret the past in the light of their new experience, he gives them a new future. They can now face Jerusalem even in the dark and they return there to share their story with the others.

They take the light of Easter Sunday back into the darkness of Good Friday, and that changes their memory. Only the risen Jesus makes sense of everything that went before. In his word and in the breaking of the bread, the past is brought up to date. The past is now reinterpreted in the light of the great truth that Jesus is Lord.

When we gather to celebrate the Eucharist we too listen to the word of God and break bread together. Jesus comes among us, not as the stranger; rather, he comes to us in word and sacrament to give us new hope to face our future with him. Our own stories may not sound very different from that of the two forlorn disciples on the road to Emmaus. We are invited, however, to understand our stories in the forgiving and everlasting light of Jesus' resurrection.

Rembrandt van Rijn, *Supper at Emmaus*

A welcoming presence

If you visit the Rembrandt House Museum in Amsterdam, you learn that Rembrandt lived in this house from 1639 until 1656, when he was declared bankrupt because he could not pay his debts. The house was in the centre of Amsterdam's Jewish community – composed mostly of Sephardic Jews who had fled Spain and Portugal during the time of the Inquisition. Rembrandt painted Supper at Emmaus in 1648 and broke with tradition by using a Jewish neighbour as his model for Jesus. In defiance of both anti-Semitism and the canonical tradition of portraying a European Jesus, Rembrandt portrays Jesus as a Jew.

Rembrandt was a student of the Bible and a Protestant: the established religion in his country was the Dutch Reformed Church. Strict Reformed theology banned images of Christ as idolatry. Rembrandt had many Lutheran, Catholic and Jewish clients and felt free to portray Jesus not only from his own lively interpretation of the Gospels but also in the light of his Jewish neighbours.

The upper part of the painting is stark and vacant; the light comes through a window in the upper left. Behind the figure of Jesus there is a monumental arch, carved from rough stone, which would not look out of place in a Romanesque basilica. The suggestion of a church apse leads the eye to interpret this table as an altar, a reading supported by the fact that the table is dressed with a heavy fringed fabric, a white cloth, reminiscent of the altar cloth and the white corporal which decorate the altar at Mass.

As Jesus breaks the *challah* bread – the Jewish braided loaf – the eyes of the two disciples are opened. The face of Christ is extraordinarily gentle, even vulnerable, as the divine radiates through his humanity, lighting up the praying hands of the disciple on the left. This is not the depiction of a distant majesty to be worshipped from afar, but the portrait of a humble host who invites us to join him at table. A dog dozes on the lower left, completing the domestic scene. We feel at home with this Jesus, at ease in his warm welcoming presence, eager to share the bread that is life.

Prayer

O Lord Jesus Christ,
on the first Easter Sunday
you joined two bewildered disciples
as they journeyed on the road to Emmaus.
You listened to the story of their experience:
how they knew you as a prophet mighty in deed and word;
you listened to the story of their expectations:
how they had hoped you would be the awaited Messiah.

Join us, dear Lord, on our roads of disappointment,
when what was once alive now appears lifeless;
when what was once appealing now seems wearisome;
when what was once sacred now looks profane.
Listen to us when we feel abandoned or betrayed,
when we are left feeling bewildered and hurt,
when our cherished hopes now seem like lost causes.

Speak to us a life-giving word,
one that helps us to understand ourselves anew,
one that enables us to see differently,
one that encourages us to hope again.
Most of all, dear Lord, welcome us to your table
so that we might be refreshed and revived
in eating the food of eternal life.

The Ascension

"And now I am sending down to you what the Father has promised.
Stay in the city then, until you are clothed with the power from on high."

Then he took them out as far as the outskirts of Bethany, and lifting up his
hands he blessed them. Now as he blessed them, he withdrew from them
and was carried up to heaven. They worshipped him and then went back to
Jerusalem full of joy; and they were continually in the Temple praising God.

(Luke 24: 49-53)

As he said this he was lifted up while they looked on, and a cloud took him
from their sight. They were still staring into the sky when suddenly two
men in white were standing near them and they said, "Why are you men
from Galilee standing here looking into the sky? Jesus who has been taken
up from you into heaven, this same Jesus will come back in the same way
as you have seen him go there."

(Acts 1:9-11)

Mission fulfilled

In the ascension we celebrate the fulfilment of Jesus' saving mission on earth and his return to his Father. Jesus, triumphant over death, has begun a new life with God the Father and will now prepare the place he promised for his friends.

While Jesus' work is completed, the work of the community he leaves behind is yet to begin. He does not charge them to go out and preach the Gospel. Instead, he instructs them: "Stay in the city, then, until you are clothed with the power from on high." In departing, Jesus leaves behind him an unfinished community. This community is powerless to re-organise or re-invent itself. They have to do something that is difficult for most of us – to stay with our poverty, to sit with our own powerlessness, to be content to wait on the gift of God. They are to wait in the absence of the one they love, funded by the belief that God's gift of the Spirit will move them to mission.

They cannot manufacture their own renewal: they have to wait for change. The disciples have already had to face dramatic change, and that experience of loss can throw us off balance. Their first loss was that of Jesus by a violent death; the second loss will be living in his physical absence now that he has gone to eternal glory as God. The one who walked beside them on the roads of Palestine, intrigued them with stories and shared meals with them – this companion will no longer be with them in the same way. Meanwhile, they wait, living in the gap, in no-man's land. They wait somewhere between grief at the loss of Jesus and hope in their own rebirth.

It is hard when someone we love is taken from us. The word "taken" accurately expresses the negative emotion of those who are left behind; the feeling of someone precious being stolen from our world; of being rendered powerless; of having to survive inside a large emptiness.

What do we do with the love that had its fulfilment in the one who is now gone? This experience of affliction is accompanied by the knowledge that there is nothing we can do to change anything. Paradoxically, the present tense is dominated by an absence. When this happens, we can end up spending our time standing and staring at the empty space once occupied by the one we love, aware only of our aching longing for the absent one who has been taken from us.

This is an image which Luke uses at the beginning of Acts: "Why are you men of Galilee standing here staring into the sky? Jesus has been taken from you…" (Acts 1:11) Jesus has indeed been taken from them. His disciples will never see him again in their lifetime. We can feel sympathy for them when we reflect on our own losses, but Jesus has to go before the Holy Spirit is sent. That gift will signal the beginning of the Church and the beginning of a new energetic mission. In the meantime the disciples have to wait and pray.

Anonymous, *The Ascension of Jesus, alabaster relief*

What now?

This stunning alabaster relief of the ascension of Jesus, in private ownership, was made in Nottingham, England, in the 15th century. From the Middle Ages alabaster was quarried in south Derbyshire and commonly used for local tombs. As the abundance of the stone became evident, different workshops were established and artists began producing reliefs and figures illustrating the lives of Christ, Mary and the saints. The colouring of the carvings was a key part of their production: they had to be brightly coloured in order to be seen from a distance and by candlelight in cathedrals and churches. This particular panel is rare, representing the few last remaining traces of English Catholic medieval art, which was mostly destroyed during the Reformation.

This relief of the ascension, with original polychrome and gilding, shows Mary and the eleven apostles as Jesus departs this earth. We see only Jesus' feet and the hem of his clothing as he returns to God from the summit of the Mount of Olives: the summit is decorated with the famous daisy pattern typical of Nottingham alabasters. Like the group of onlookers we are privileged to view the final moment of Jesus on earth: he is already entering the glory of heaven and will be forever lost to sight.

Mary kneels in prayer whilst, opposite her, the beardless Beloved Disciple waves a goodbye with his right hand whilst he holds a palm in his left hand. Behind him the kneeling St Jude, carrying his emblem of a boat, looks upwards at the departure. Interestingly, it is the group left behind, rather than Jesus' leave-taking, that forms the focus of this panel.

When we look at them, we might well wonder: when they turn to one another, what will they do now that he is gone? How will they bear up? Will their memories of him be conflicting? Will they argue about what he really meant? How will they manage their differences? Will they agree on what they should be doing in his name and who exactly should be doing what? Will they become side-lined by peripheral concerns? How will they preserve his memory? Will they face the future with confidence? These continue to be our questions in the Church today.

Prayer

Father in heaven,
we ask that you stretch our imaginations
to sense the majesty and mystery
of the ascension of your beloved Son.

Your loving Christ once dwelt on earth,
confined by time and space.
He walked the hills of his familiar Galilee
and fished the lake with his disciples.
He left his home-place to risk himself
in another world, in the city streets of Jerusalem.
Throughout all his journeying
he rubbed shoulders with so many people,
listening to their stories, noticing their pain,
all the time sharing his love and insight.
He ended up sharing his very life.

Let his kind of love be a model for us,
an outreach to others in trust and humility.
Give us faith to discern in every time and place
his continuing presence among us,
particularly in those who are poor and hungry,
in those who suffer estrangement,
in all those who are sick in body or spirit.

You took Christ home, beyond our sight,
so that we might seek him anew in those around us.
May we follow where he has led
and find our hope in his glory,
for he is Lord, this day and forever.

The Descent of the Holy Spirit

When Pentecost day came round, they had all met in one room, when suddenly they heard what sounded like a powerful wind from heaven, the noise of which filled the entire house in which they were sitting; and something appeared to them that seemed like tongues of fire; these separated and came to rest on the head of each of them. They were all filled with the Holy Spirit, and began to speak foreign languages as the Spirit gave them the gift of speech.

Now there were devout men living in Jerusalem from every nation under heaven, and at this sound they all assembled, each one bewildered to hear these men speaking his own language. They were amazed and astonished. "Surely," they said, "all these men speaking are Galileans? How does it happen that each of us hears them in his own native language? Parthians, Medes and Elamites; people from Mesopotamia, Judaea and Cappadocia, Pontus and Asia, Phrygia and Pamphylia, Egypt and the parts of Libya round Cyrene; as well as visitors from Rome – Jews and proselytes alike – Cretans and Arabs; we hear them preaching in our own language about the marvels of God."

Everyone was amazed and unable to explain it; they asked one another what it all meant. Some, however, laughed it off. "They have been drinking too much new wine," they said.

(Acts 2:1-13)

The language of the Spirit

Luke writes, "They had all met in one room" – not only the twelve apostles but also a larger group which included followers and family. The room is probably the same place where the Last Supper was held. In all likelihood there is a measure of fear, since the group might be afraid they will suffer the same punishment as Jesus endured at the hands of the authorities. In this sacred enclosure they are safe from the interference of the outside world.

In contrast there is the powerful image of the Holy Spirit as one who is not shy of the boundaries and the barriers that people build. He is not halted by locked doors or locked hearts. He does not exclude himself from the restrictive areas in which people settle. When the Spirit comes, it is not like a spring breeze that whispers unnoticed through a room; it is more like a hurricane that lays flat all the precious protections that people construct. And the Spirit takes this group of followers and fires them with a new energy, a new enthusiasm and a new authority.

The presence of the Spirit makes the group open their lives to others. They do not just decorate their sacred enclosure: they leave it and pass over into the lives of other people with the gifts of Gospel and peace and forgiveness. They all go outdoors. They move to the marketplace where people gather and there the apostles proclaim to all the power of the Gospel. They tell a Magnificat and proclaim how God has worked wonders in them.

Luke explores two reactions by the crowd. Some people think that the apostles are drunk – no doubt because they're sure it takes some kind of spirit to transform these men. Whatever it is, everyone acknowledges that something dramatic happened to change the outlook and behaviour of the followers of Jesus. The name of that experience is Spirit.

Another reaction is a joyous one when people realise that the apostles are speaking their language. Perhaps we have all heard people say to us in a mixture of relief and enthusiasm: "Now you're speaking my language!" When that happens there is communion, where before there had only been misunderstanding and division. The apostles break through to people because they preach in the deep language that is in all of us and which is rarely spoken. It is the language in search of understanding; it is music in search of a melody; it is the language of the Spirit.

The language of the Spirit speaks in the grammar of forgiveness and love and understanding. It is one that everyone understands and needs to hear. It is the true language of the Gospel – one that has no boundaries and no special dictionaries are needed to understand it. Of course not all preaching is as effective as the apostolic accomplishment at Pentecost, but it is the same Spirit that continues to inspire the preaching of the Gospel today.

The priest/poet David Scott imagines a preacher today, worrying about the effectiveness of what he is doing and taking solace in the fond hope that when he looks at his collected old sermons on the shelf:

> …As the spiral notebooks rust
> along the shelves, who knows how a word
> in the thickest of the sermon's stickiest part,
> might just have winged its way into the heart
> of one young stranger there, and taken roost.

David Scott, *"The Priest in the Pulpit"* in *Beyond the Drift: New and Selected Poems*

Unknown Portuguese artist, *Pentecost*

"The Church is a woman"

This anonymous painting, dated around 1550, is now in the Alberto Museum, Guimarães, Portugal. It depicts the fire of the Holy Spirit at Pentecost reaching out and enlightening the waiting assembly; it includes an unidentified monk/patron in the right foreground. Unlike other paintings that depict the gift of the Spirit, this painting has a more ecumenical feel to it. Luke's inner circle at the beginning of the Church (Acts 1:12-14) has three groups who gather together in prayer. Together, and only together, can they witness to the entirety of the Jesus story:

> ■ The named apostles who cover Jesus' public ministry until the passion; they also witness the appearances of the risen Jesus. ■ The women of Galilee who cover the passion, the death and burial of Jesus, and the empty tomb. ■ Mary and the brothers of Jesus who cover the early life of Jesus.

As the woman Mary was "first at the cradle", so the women of Galilee are "last at the cross". These women are moved from the limits of the Jesus story – the beginning and the end – and placed at the centre of the infant Church.

The presence of these women at the heart of the Church is beautifully represented in this painting. Central to the whole group is the seated Mary (almost enthroned), hands formed in prayer, reading from a prayer book open on her knees. Behind Mary are three of the women of Galilee, all kneeling, just like the remainder of the group. To Mary's right, in the foreground, is her new son, the beardless Beloved Disciple, a picture of prayerful attentiveness.

This is not an exclusive all-male enclave, but an inclusive celebration of the original witnesses of Luke's Gospel story now inflamed and anointed by the Holy Spirit to demonstrate in their own lives the power of the Gospel. As Pope Francis said in his address, *Women Called to Serve, not to Servitude*: "It pleases me to think that the Church is not *il Chiesa* ('the Church', masculine): it is *la Chiesa* (feminine). The Church is a woman! The Church is a mother! And that's beautiful, isn't it? We have to think deeply about this…Even in the Church, it is important to ask oneself: what presence does the woman have?"

Prayer

Almighty and gracious Father,
we pray for the Church in every part of the world:
that the Spirit will continue to renew each community.
Open our hearts to your truth and love.
Stir us to new mission in sharing the Gospel.

We pray for the Spirit of unity to dwell in the Church:
that the wounds of division which mark the Body of Christ
and continue to hurt it will be healed;
that all peoples can come together
and with one voice give glory to you, our one Father.

We pray that the members of the Church throughout the world
will learn the powerful language of the Spirit of God:
that we will speak it especially to those
who never hear tender words of love and peace.

We pray in gratitude for all women in the Church
and for all who progress the spirit and the work of the Gospel:
that they will experience appreciation for their particular gifts
and live in the respect and encouragement of the community.

Almighty and gracious Father,
continue to pour our your Spirit on us,
especially on those who live in dark places.
May your Spirit carry faith to the doubting,
strength to the weak,
solace to those who mourn.
And may your blessing abide with us
now and evermore.

The Assumption of the Blessed Virgin Mary into Heaven

And Mary said:

> "My soul proclaims the greatness of the Lord
> and my spirit exults in God my saviour;
> because he has looked upon his lowly handmaid.
> Yes, from this day forward, all generations will call me blessed,
> for the Almighty has done great things for me.
> Holy is his name,
> and his mercy reaches from age to age for those who fear him.
> He has shown the power of his arm,
> he has routed the proud of heart.
> He has pulled down princes from their thrones
> and exalted the lowly.
> The hungry he has filled with good things,
> the rich sent empty away.
> He has come to the help of Israel his servant,
> mindful of his mercy
> – according to the promise he made to our ancestors –
> of his mercy to Abraham and to his descendants for ever."

(Luke 1:46-55)

"For the Almighty has done great things for me"

It is worth noting that the belief in the assumption of Mary had its origin in the popular faith of the people. Christians could not believe that Mary's body underwent decay after being separated from her soul at death. They could not imagine that her body would disintegrate after the unique role she played in sacred history. The faithful came to believe that Mary was bodily assumed into heaven, thus guaranteeing that she was present with God, body and soul.

Just as devout Jews envisioned the death of Moses as a grace-filled event in which angels carried his body to God, so Christians began describing the death of Mary as her return to God. What the New Testament did not supply, an imaginative faith readily provided. So images abounded of Mary being assumed into heaven and crowned queen. Artists and poets vied with each other in expressing images of the heavenly scenes. Hence the paintings which adorn so many art galleries around the world: legions of chubby angels conveying Mary on a celestial flight; saintly choirs celebrating her arrival with motets; baroque coronation scenes so grand that even the Trinity can only look on in wonder.

We may smile at these adventures in faith, but they were inspired by a love of Mary which insisted that nothing on earth or in heaven could overstate the importance of the mother of the Son of the Most High God. The assumption of Mary also points to what we believe God will do for us. We believe that our whole person, body and soul, will be raised to a new existence in the peace of God. This is what the dogmatic definition tells us as it expresses the hope "that faith in the bodily assumption of Mary into heaven may make our faith in our resurrection both stronger and more active".

Mary's importance is not limited to giving us hope about the afterlife: she gives every Christian hope in the growing struggle of everyday life. In Luke's Gospel Mary is portrayed as the one who glorifies God because "the Almighty has done great things for me". She is a woman of the people, whose song delights in God's choice of her, whose spirit soars because God has not overlooked this lowly handmaid. But she is also a dangerous woman because she is the one who voices the subversive hope of the poor and the little ones:

> He has pulled down princes from their thrones
>   and exalted the lowly.
> The hungry he has filled with good things,
>   the rich sent empty away.

In the *Magnificat* we see Mary as a radical woman. She is the woman who hungers for a new justice on earth, one that reflects the justice of God. The God who did not overlook her is the God who dethrones the mighty and exalts the lowly. In this dispensation the hungry are filled with good things, the rich sent empty away. Mary voices a contrary wisdom. That contrary wisdom is now a powerful voice in heaven. We celebrate Mary assumed into heaven as the protector of all who are oppressed and overlooked and scorned.

Titian, *The Assumption of the Virgin*

Going home

When you walk in to the Frari in Venice you immediately see Titian's early masterpiece over the high altar. Set in a frame that looks like a triumphal arch, it was painted between 1516 and 1518. It stands almost twenty-three feet high and dominates the basilica, dedicated to the assumption under the title of Santa Maria Gloriosa. Titian completed the work when he was twenty-eight years old.

The Assumption of the Virgin was Titian's first commission by the city of Venice. Heaven and earth meet one another in this painting. There are three tiers: the first is occupied by the apostles, the second by Mary and the arc of putti, the third by God the Father and his two assistants. The composition of the painting leads the eyes ever upwards, beginning with the red-robed apostles at the bottom, to Mary's billowing red dress, and finally to the red cloak of God the Father.

The apostles are grounded, their looks and gestures a mixture of agitation and devotion. Mary's eyes look upwards, not downwards, her arms open in receptivity to the glory that awaits her. The figure of God the Father hovers; his arms open in a welcoming gesture, his right hand ready to take the waiting crown for Mary. Titian has chosen brilliant golden hues which turn a dazzling white at the centre to denote the heavenly space Mary will now share with God.

For such a monumental painting, there is a surprising intimacy and warmth about it. As Mary's eyes are focused on God, his loving gaze welcomes her to her true home. The young woman who once proclaimed: "The Almighty has done great things for me," now experiences the everlasting glory of those words.

Prayer

Almighty and everlasting Father,
who endued with singular grace
the Mother of our Lord:
we bless you for taking Mary home to yourself,
and for acknowledging and celebrating
her unique role in the story of salvation.

We pray for the universal Church
which is blessed with Mary as mother:
that it will always proclaim the greatness of God
and faithfully preach the message of Christ Jesus.

We bring before your merciful presence
all mothers and grandmothers:
that you will continue to bless them
and the fruit of their womb.

Look with mercy, O Lord our God,
on all who struggle in poverty
and for all those who are persecuted:
that you will again show the power of your arm
and bring down the powers that tyrannise people
while cherishing all who hunger for what is right.

We bring before you
the multitudes of refugees throughout the world:
that, in your mercy, you will save them from despair,
from disappointment and from bitterness of spirit.
Bless those who struggle for their relief and security
and hold them close to your heart.

The Coronation of the Blessed Virgin Mary

After that I saw a huge number, impossible to count, of people from every nation, race, tribe and language; they were standing in front of the throne and in front of the Lamb, dressed in white robes and holding palms in their hands. They shouted aloud, "Victory to our God, who sits on the throne, and to the Lamb!"

And all the angels who were standing in a circle round the throne, surrounding the elders and the four animals, prostrated themselves before the throne, and touched the ground with their foreheads, worshipping God with these words, "Amen. Praise and glory and wisdom and thanksgiving and honour and power and strength to our God for ever and ever. Amen."…

Now a great sign appeared in heaven: a woman, adorned with the sun, standing on the moon, and with the twelve stars on her head for a crown.

(Revelation 7:9-12; 12:1)

Crowning glory

This final decade of the Rosary celebrates an event outside the limits of recorded history and time, one not registered in early Christian literature: when Mary, the humble handmaid of the Lord who became the Mother of God is crowned queen in heaven. Like the assumption, this is an example of the imaginative faith of the people supplying what the dogmatic tradition was silent on.

In the Book of Revelation the woman with twelve stars on her head as a crown is often interpreted as an image of Mary. The twelve stars represent each of the twelve tribes of Israel whose entire history led to the moment we celebrate at the beginning of the Rosary, the Annunciation. When Mary readily submitted herself to the will of God, she could not have known what God had in store for her – not the heartaches and not the sorrows; certainly not the glory. At times, as she pondered all of these things in her heart, she might well have wondered where this journey might lead. Perhaps she even questioned herself if she could bear the burden and press on to the end.

Yet her faith remained steadfast and she did indeed persevere. And now the crown is placed upon her head in an act of solemn recognition of her fidelity and generosity of spirit. Again this is a sign of hope for all God's faithful people: where Mary goes we hope to follow, so her crown is a symbol of the crown of sainthood that awaits all of us, if we heed her example by following her Son.

In the Litany of Loreto, named after its place of origin, Loreto, Italy, where it was recorded as early as 1558, Mary is celebrated as:

Queen of Angels,
Queen of Patriarchs,
Queen of Prophets,
Queen of Apostles,
Queen of Martyrs,
Queen of Confessors,
Queen of Virgins,
Queen of all Saints,
Queen conceived without original sin,
Queen assumed into heaven,
Queen of the most holy Rosary,
Queen of families,
Queen of peace.

At the conclusion of the Rosary, we celebrate how God blesses and celebrates Mary of Nazareth as she is crowned in heaven: a unique honour for an unmatched life of love and loyalty. We conclude our Rosary by acknowledging Mary as "Queen of the most holy Rosary".

Luca Signorelli, *The Coronation of the Virgin*

An intimate moment

Luca Signorelli was born around 1442 in the town of Cortona in the region of Tuscany. Although he worked on commissions in palaces and cathedrals in Siena and Orvieto and Rome – he has one painting in the Sistine Chapel – he always returned to Cortona, where he felt most at ease. He was celebrated in his lifetime as much for his humanity as for his art – as a man of sincerity and courtesy, full of kindliness and understanding. *The Coronation of the Virgin* was painted around 1508 for the church of San Francesco, Arcevia, in the province of Ancona, and it now hangs in the San Diego Museum of Art.

The kneeling Mary lowers her eyes in modesty and reverence as she nervously arranges her fingers into the form of praying hands; she inclines her head forwards to accept the crown from her son. The colours of her clothes – red and green and blue – match those worn by Jesus, as does her hair. The bearded and long-haired Jesus is about to place the crown he holds on the head of his mother. Eyes fixed on Mary's hands, he seems to be pausing momentarily for his mother to arrange her hands in the proper position.

The figure of God the Father is represented as a dignified old man wearing a golden cloak, stretching out his arms to embrace and bless both Jesus and Mary. You get the impression that as soon as the crown has landed, his hands will press the shoulders of Jesus and Mary in approval. Two putti hover and look on behind his shoulders. Behind Mary and Jesus the heavenly choir is limited to two angels playing their instruments. The dove representing the Holy Spirit and completing the Trinity is surprisingly missing.

Compared to the majority of paintings of the coronation of the Virgin, Signorelli's is modest and intimate. It does not display a spectacle in a crowded heavenly court with hundreds of attendant saints and trumpeting angels. Rather, it focuses more on a domestic scene of signal importance for heaven and earth – the recognition of Mary's role in the story of salvation and her queenly role in heaven. This is our humble mother, now our queen.

135

Prayer

Salve Regina

Salve, Regina, Mater misericordiæ,
vita, dulcedo, et spes nostra, salve.
Ad te clamamus exsules filii Hevæ,
Ad te suspiramus, gementes et flentes
in hac lacrimarum valle.
Eia, ergo, advocata nostra, illos tuos
misericordes oculos ad nos converte;
Et Jesum, benedictum fructum ventris tui,
nobis post hoc exsilium ostende.
O clemens, O pia, O dulcis Virgo Maria.

Hail, holy Queen, Mother of Mercy,
hail our life, our sweetness and our hope.
To thee do we cry, poor banished children of Eve;
to thee do we send up our sighs,
mourning and weeping in this valley of tears.
Turn then, most gracious advocate,
thine eyes of mercy toward us;
and after this our exile,
show unto us the blessed fruit of thy womb, Jesus.
O clement, O loving, O sweet Virgin Mary.